WHAT IS AMERICAN LITERATURE?

ILAN STAVANS

WHAT IS AMERICAN LITERATURE?

OXFORD
UNIVERSITY PRESS

OXFORD

UNIVERSITY PRESS

Great Clarendon Street, Oxford, OX2 6DP,
United Kingdom

Oxford University Press is a department of the University of Oxford.
It furthers the University's objective of excellence in research, scholarship,
and education by publishing worldwide. Oxford is a registered trade mark of
Oxford University Press in the UK and in certain other countries

First Edition published in 2022

Impression: 1

Published in the United States of America by Oxford University Press
198 Madison Avenue, New York, NY 10016, United States of America

British Library Cataloguing in Publication Data
Data available

Library of Congress Control Number: 2021941664

ISBN 978–0–19–881621–8

Printed and bound by
CPI Group (UK) Ltd, Croydon, CR0 4YY

To Steven G. Kellman

PREFACE

American Carnage

I am in quarantine, along with millions of Americans, and, beyond national borders, with almost every human alive. A pandemic is ravaging the globe. It is having a particularly pernicious effect in the United States. More people have died than battle deaths during the Civil War. The richest, most powerful country in history, an economic engine to the world, a beacon of ideas, has been brought to its knees.

Yet kneeling these days—not to bow down to nationalist iconography—is also a sign of rebellion.

Like everything else, responses to Covid-19 have polarized Americans. The Northeast, the site of early hot spots, was meticulous in its response: masks, hands sanitation, six feet of separation, protective gear. The infection rates were soon brought down. But in the South and the West, libertarians and others have stood up to health experts and state officials to claim their civil liberties were being infringed. Since when should the government tell individuals what to do?

Amidst the calamity, police brutality against people of color runs rampant. And, with the death-by-suffocation, on May 25, 2020, after 9 minutes and 29 seconds, of George Floyd, a 46-year-old Black man in Minneapolis, Minnesota, seismic upheaval has swept the American streets, and, soon after, countless cities planet-wide.

"Black Lives Matter!"—furious, exhausted marchers chant in the largest protest movement ever to take shape in the United States.

Systemic racism is the target. Change must be swift. White America is on its way out the door. In a country that sees itself as an experiment, a new, more diverse and pluralistic face is finally coming together. Confederate statues are being brought down. And many more: Christopher Columbus is out; so is conquistador and New Mexico governor Juan de Oñate, infamously known for the Acoma massacre of 1599, in which between eight hundred and a thousand indigenous people died. At the entrance of the Museum of Natural History in New York City, the statue of Teddy Roosevelt, the bigoted twenty-sixth president, riding on his horse with a slave and a Native America submissively on each side, is being moved to an undisclosed storage location.

The Founding Fathers, most of whom were slave-owners, aren't immune. Are they next? Should Washington, D.C., change its name? A *villa miseria*, a belt of poverty surrounding the hallways of power, should it become a state? And is the American constitution better served in the dumpster?

Is all this a new beginning? Or is it the end?

Meanwhile, at the helm of this dystopia has been President Donald J. Trump, the egomaniac TV personality turned racist-in-chief, whose mantra at his inauguration was "American carnage." The age of disruption has triumphantly arrived; the "deep state" cannot be allowed to set the rules. Trump's rhetoric is nothing if not incendiary: divide and conquer, ridicule the losers, make room for the country as a big corporation.

Trump's legacy, in his own words, would be an amusement park honoring American heroes, his own handsome statue forever at its center.

Is there a better time to talk literature? No other intellectual endeavor in my eyes is a better window to scrutinize human contradictions. And none other looks at the tension between individual and society with equal zest.

The nation's literature has always encouraged probing questions: Where did the idea of America as exceptional come from? Is that exceptionalism still current? And what keeps Americans reinventing themselves? Is the literature they have produced exceptional too? Might it be said to constitute their collective memory? How is that memory transmitted across generations? Or is America grown too distracted to even notice it has a memory?

From the get-go, American literature has been about the idea of home, starting with William Bradford's journal *Of Plymouth Plantation* to Phillis Wheatley's poetry and Olaudah Equiano's autobiography *The Interesting Narrative*, Washington Irving's "Rip Van Winkle" and James Fenimore Cooper's adventure about the frontiersman Natty Bumppo called the *Leatherstocking Tales*. And even before then, the indigenous oral traditions. Indeed, at the fateful moment of birth the encounter between the indigenous population rooted in the land and a bunch of renegade settlers convinced they were given that land by a righteous Almighty showcases an all-consuming clash of civilizations. This clash would eventually antagonize individualists and collectivists, and nativists and globalists. As is crystal clear from the vantage moment in which I'm writing, the friction between them still propels the country forward.

The nation's literature is as much about pursuing the proverbial American Dream as it is about dissenting from it. At its heart are Huckleberry Finn and Jim, a pair of outcasts, one a 13-year-old boy, the other a runaway slave, looking for freedom and a place for themselves in a society that sees them as a threat. Through their itinerant adventures, they survey the Mississippi environment, natural and human, using a makeshift language—American English—that, like an accordion, expands and contorts as they react to one challenge after another.

As Ernest Hemingway once put it (and I agree wholeheartedly), Huck and Jim are ground zero in American literature. Every character before and after is in dialogue with their odyssey.

To think dynamically about American books—fiction and nonfiction, poetry, theater, and translations—one must read realistically as well as allusively. For at its core this literature is nothing but about the lab where democracy gets tested. It opens readers' eyes and it blinds them; it builds alternative universes where American can see its face reflected. It encourages political participation and also puts people to sleep. All at once, it propels change and manufactures consent.

The severity of Covid-19, unquestionably the most important historical event of my lifetime, has exposed deep fault lines in America. The past feels less settled than before. There is anxiety about solvency and about the concept of home. Elites are afraid of large masses of people awakening in a vengeful spirit.

What follows is an assortment of reflections by a compulsive reader on how America manufactures consent and rebellion. I'm not interested in traditional criticism, which to me smells of Ivory Tower snobbery. I'm interested in literature as a window to life. What do books say about us? Do they carry our DNA? Or else, do they teach us how to live?

Needless to say, I realize the enormity of these questions. And the subjectivity they entail. One reader's enthusiastic response to *Adventures of Huckleberry Finn* is in sharp contrast with another reader's outright rejection. But that is precisely why literature matters: because it is always personal.

These meditations, therefore, are an introduction to American literature. Obviously, all introductions are biased. Mine is a kind of autobiography of my reading habits. This is how I answer the question: What is American literature? This is also how American literature reads me.

To suggest that that literature is vast, multifaceted, and uncontainable is to state the obvious.

Getting a handle of it, therefore, is like putting together a jigsaw puzzle. I have organized my response into four chapters in total, each divided into five sections. The chapters are thematic in scope and within that frame, chronological in historical order.

The first chapter reflects on America as a nation without a past and how the nation's literature addresses that absence. It discusses, again from the viewpoint of texts, the birth that gave place to the United States as symbolized by the indigenous population and repurposed by the British settlers. It also looks at the role God was said to play in that origin from Ralph Waldo Emerson's "On Self-Reliance" to Alice Walker's *The Color Purple*. It discusses the disregard for indigenous literary voices, then moves on to W. E. B. Du Bois's *The Souls of Black Folk* and discusses slavery as an original sin.

This chapter also points to Emma Lazarus's sonnet "The New Colossus," engraved in a plaque in the pedestal of the Statue of Liberty, that once welcomed immigrants to America with an allusive—though at that time still elusive—dream. To this effect, I bring in the work of a couple of successful immigrants whose literary quests involved, among other things, switching languages: Isaac Bashevis Singer and Vladimir Nabokov. And against the backdrop of Emily Dickinson's poem "I'm Nobody! Who are you?," *Little Women*, and *The Great Gatsby*, it discusses the concept of exceptionalism and the philosophy of individualism.

Onward to the second chapter, which deals with permutations of American individualism, from runaways Huck and Jim to border jumpers like Gregorio Cortez and other subversives. It looks at kids' lit (especially Maurice Sendak's *Where the Wild Things Are* and the carnivalesque universe of Dr. Seuss). It engages in an exploration of American borders, materialism, and the insistence on owning things. The chapter highlights the tradition of protest in American literature from Henry David Thoreau and James Baldwin to Américo Paredes to Betty Friedan, and beyond. It talks about the way the body is hypersexualized from Walt Whitman to Tony Kushner.

I talk about language in the third chapter, starting with the insistence of newness that must permeate everything, especially young adult fiction series like *The Hardy Boys* and *The Hunger Games*. I meditate on the role of dictionaries in America (most crucially Noah Webster's *An American Dictionary of the English Language*) and the lack of an institution like *L'Académie française* in the United States. All this is seen through the lens of the anti-intellectual tradition that marks American life since the beginning. I also talk of the uses and abuses of American English, focusing on "irrelevant" items like the exclamation mark and the ellipsis.

I move on in the chapter to the friction between high- and low-brow culture, and literature in particular, concentrating on detective and science fiction. To achieve this, I use as my point of departure a famous comment by *New Yorker* critic Edmund Wilson. And I engage in a discussion of melodrama in "formulaic" literature. I then move to assess the role of literary critics and their style, at times crystalline, at other times obfuscatingly dense, and the disinterest in them among twenty-first-century audiences. And I tackle the pervasive quality of auto-correctors in smart phones and their impact on reader's attention for literary endeavors.

The intercourse between democracy and literature is the traction that moves the fifth chapter. I approach books as merchandise, celebrate the way American libraries—cool places—have reinvented themselves since the Second World War, meditate on teaching literature today after a thirty-plus-year career, and analyze the maligned "3 percent," which is the amount of foreign books translated into English every year. And in the last part I return to Covid-19 and Black Lives Matter in 2020 by commenting on Langston Hughes's deeply felt protest poem "Let America Be America Again," contrasting it with F. Scott Fitzgerald's optimism in his meditative book *This Side of Paradise*.

Finally, in an epilogue that looks into the future I imagine a new American literature that comes about after the Second American Civil War (2023–7), one as plentiful as the oeuvre of the cadre of authors that resulted after the first one. It is here, finally, where the quest to answer the question "What is American literature?" finds something resembling a resolution.

My intention on this occasion isn't to do close readings of texts; instead, it is to look at authors as guides to understand the ripening of the idea of America, following their lead by encouraging a sweeping overview of the literary canon that is yoked together by concept rather than temporality, field, ethnicity, and genre. I hope the gathering of such diverse voices has the potential to disrupt how we read, if not what we read. While the assembly of authors might at times feel to some ad hoc and even dizzying, the organizing logic of each section is based on stream of consciousness. In other words, my purpose is to understand how certain texts, alone and in unlikely partnerships, grapple with questions of alienation, language, and home. The lexicon and value system I employ is built on the premise that fiction in its essence isn't only unstable but subject to endless interpretations. Each reading of that fiction is an appropriation. Literary criticism isn't a science; nor does it need to be schematic. Instead, it should do what literature itself does: be jazzy, reacting to life spontaneously, as it happens, and not as if it had been stored in a lab.

To various degrees, all these chapters are infused by, and respond to, the havoc the Trump era represents: the abysmal disparities between the small number of haves and the countless have-nots; the bottlenecked ERs where doctors, handcuffed by shortages of equipment and medicine, must decide who lives and who dies; the winding roads leading to food kitchens; the under-performing schools where children are set to fail; and the roach-, rat-, drug-, and gun-infested cities were the American Dream goes sour.

It isn't a pretty picture. Oscar Wilde once suggested—or was it George Bernard Shaw? Georges Clemenceau? Winston Churchill? The quote is exquisite to such degree it is attributed to any number of sources—that America is the only country that went from bar-barism to decadence without civilization in between. As Covid-19 ravages it without mercy, it is a nation in fear.[1] The influenza

---

[1] Regarding fear, two things are clear from the current viral onslaught: the first is that we are paralyzed by an unshakeable sense of terror; and the second is that, while such prime emotion feels new and untamable, it is as old as humankind.

We fear what we cannot control: the collapse of routine; being among the unlucky who die; the wrath of nature is upon us. In *Henry VI* (1592), Shakespeare says: "Of all based passions, fear is the most accursed." It is an animalistic reaction in the face of danger. Our heart beats at a faster pace. We feel anxious, trapped, and we doubt our capacity to reason.

On the surface, it might not appear to do us any good that literature is filled with retorts to calamities. Yet literature is the catalogue, factual and imaginative, we have built to understand what others before us have done while in a state of desperation. Floods, famine, and destruction abound in the bible; and, of course, the bible is always used as bouncing board to explain the present. The prophets of doom are saying now, as they did when Sodom and Gomora were annihilated, that Covid-19 is punishment for collective reckless. The same goes for the twin brothers who are the protagonists of *Popol Vuh*, the Maya K'iche' book of creation; they are overtaken by disasters macabrely ordered on them by the evil lords of Xibalba.

More matter-of-fact depictions of widespread chaos generated by pestilence appear in the *Decameron* as Florence, like Venice today, is left deserted by the Black Death, and in Daniel Defoe's *Journal of the Plague Year*, which gives a minute-by-minute CNN-like report of London in 1665 as it is ravished by the bubonic fever. And in Michael Crichton's techno-thriller *The Andromeda Strain*, which undoubtedly feels closer to our dystopian present (ironically, I watched the 1971 movie adaptation not long ago and these days I can't get it out of my dreams), an out-of-space microbe decimates the population of Arizona.

But fear is also a creative stimulant. According to Spinoza, who in the seventeenth century made, in his book *Ethics*, the best, most complete list of our emotions, with explanations on how they function, is a compliment of fear. There is no *hope* unmingled with *fear* and vice versa, he proclaimed. Through ingenuity, we imagine ourselves out of despair.

A small group of characters in Jose Saramago's *Blindness* (1995) are caught in an asylum in which they have been quarantined as they escape into the apocalyptic world outside, led by the doctor's wife (Saramago masterfully refers to his characters not by name but by their prime social role) in search of shelter. By the end of the novel, they have built a commune when the absence of sight in the general population vanishes as mysteriously as it appeared. What we readers are left with isn't sheer doom; instead, we are invited to recognize the stunning human capacity to metastasize fear into hope.

And in *One Hundred Years of Solitude* (1967), José Arcadio Buendía, the family patriarch, understanding the impact insomnia is likely to have on everyone, realizes forgetfulness will soon strike like thunder and lightning on people because to remember our mind needs sleep. Resourceful as he is—part scientist, part mystic—he imposes a strategy so that reality doesn't collapse altogether: he and others put signs on objects, the word "caw" attached to a cow, so that the Macondinos remember what it is. But the illness is so inclement in its sweep, José Arcadio decides to attach descriptions to objects: a cow is milked twice a day; the

pandemic (1918–19), also known as 'Spanish Flu" although it likely didn't start in Spain, overlapped with the end of the First World War. It killed an estimated 50 million people worldwide, 675,000 of them in the United States.

It left a deep imprint in literature. T. S. Eliot, D. H. Lawrence, Mary McCarthy, Raymond Chandler, and Dashiell Hammett, among others, fell ill from it. Hemingway's *Death in the Afternoon* (1932) deals with it, as do Katherine Anne Porter's novella *Pale Horse, Pale Rider* (1939), William Carlos William's *The Autobiography of William Carlos Williams* (1948), and McCarthy's *Memories of a Catholic Girlhood* (1957). Something of the same caliber, if not more strident, will come out from the Covid-19 tragedy.

That's because the current picture is a phantasmagorical vision worthy of Pieter *Brueghel* the *Elder*. Hospitals are at record capacity, with provisions running low. Patients are being turned away from help, pushing doctors into the role of deciding who should live and who should die. Nurses and other first responders feel drained. Masks are used unevenly. Plots by white supremacists to kidnap state governors in order to start a civil war that would lead to societal collapse have been uncovered, roiling the political landscape.

milk is used to drink; it is particularly nutritive for children; and so on. To the degree possible, this approach allows life to feel anchored.

Although it is being repeated to exhaustion, nothing currently affecting us is truly unprecedented. Plagues are a sine qua non of civilizations. Scores will die; the majority will survive, although not unscathed. Each epoch, each culture displays different answers. Some might become more religious. Others may break out into song. Shakespeare wrote *King Lear* during a plague in England; Sor Juana Inés de La Cruz, the best poet Latin America ever produced, fell silent, for a variety of reasons, as the plague hit her Mexico convent. The two, it is fair to say, were irrevocably touched by their circumstance.

I edited a volume called *And We Came Outside and Saw the Stars Again: Writers from Around the World on the Covid-19 Pandemic* (New York: Restless Books, 2020).

Businesses large and small have gone bankrupt. Unemployment has skyrocketed. One in five children goes hungry. Schools have opted for online learning, pushing the instruction onto already fatigued parents. The sense of isolation is widespread. A third of Americans are anxious, depressed, and disillusioned. Rumors and conspiracies are the order of the day. Was all this planned ahead of time? The promise of a federally approved vaccine is on the horizon but still appears remote. Will it work? Will people be suspicious of it? Are pharmacological corporations using it as a tool of control?

The disconsolate state of America during this pandemic should not be the sole prism through which to appreciate its creativity. American literature is a Borgesian Aleph: it is multifarious in form and splendorous in reach, embracing tradition while looking for renewal and finding ecstasy in unexpected places. To imagine Whitman, Dickinson, Du Bois, Bashevis Singer, Elizabeth Bishop, Allen Ginsberg, Baldwin, Susan Sontag, Paredes, and Toni Morrison having a beer together is to me a delicious picture.

This brazen book is that picture. Born out of fury, it is my reading—critical, anecdotal—of America now.

Like *Peronismo* in Argentina and *Chavismo* in Venezuela (yes, the U.S. is now, finally, part of the Latin American community of nations), *Trumpismo* is a toxic cult-of-personality political movement whose effects are unpredictable. The fact that Trump, whose lexicon included the word "loser" only in so far as it applied to others, refusal to concede after the presidential election solidified the false conviction by a large number of his 70-million base that the results were rigged. This brought about a slippery slope that further divided the American people.

In spite of their incompatibilities, what unites them isn't just the coincidence of place. It is hope. Even in an age of calamity, hope is an angel whose visits make children smile. In the middle of the pandemic, a small restaurant in a rural Upstate New York town put out a street sign: "Trying Times Are Times for Trying."

November 28, 2020

CONTENTS

"Democracy is the pathetic belief in the collective wisdom of individual ignorance."

H. L. Mencken, *Notes on Democracy* (1926)

CHAPTER I

THE AMBITION OF ORIGINS

1. Manifest Destiny

America is a country without a past. Or better, with an endlessly recyclable past. William Faulkner said that in the United States, "the past is never dead. It's not even the past."[1]

The ambition of origins remains open-ended. Please come inside and find the past you're most comfortable with! Yes, come to this land of possibilities. Nowhere else will you be the person you've always dreamed of. You'll get your personal kit at the entrance. It's easy to handle. Build your own past at leisure; no one will question you. You're in charge of your own fate.

To a large extent, that cornucopia of possibilities is the result of America being a country of newcomers, a country made of escapees from other places always starting anew. Their combined objective is to build a new home. Not only a house but a home, at once individual and collective.

In that pursuit, legend has it that first came the settlers, better called Pilgrims. Look at it in William Bradford's journals

---

[1] The line comes from Faulkner's novel *Requiem for a Nun*, published in 1951. My source is William Faulkner, *Novels 1942–1954: Go Down, Moses / Intruder in the Dust / Requiem for a Nun / A Fable* (New York: Library of America, 1994). It is one of the most frequently repeated quotes in America, part of the nation's wisdom database. In 2012, the Faulkner estate sued Woody Allen for misquoting it in his film *Midnight in Paris* (2011). A judge dismissed the case.

from 1630 to 1651, known as *Of Plymouth Plantation*. Though not chronologically the first publication in the nation's literary shelf, it is the foundational account, from the perspective of Europeans, the scaffolding on which the edifice of American identity would be built.

Bradford and his cohorts are portrayed as heroic refugees. "All great and honorable actions are accompanied with great difficulties," Bradford argues, "and both must be enterprised and overcome with answerable courage." The Almighty gave them permission and they embraced the mission. He wonders, proudly:

> May not and ought not the children of these fathers rightly say: "Our fathers were Englishmen which came over this great ocean, and were ready to perish in this wilderness but they cried unto the Lord, and He heard their voice, and looked on their adversity, &c. Let them therefore praise the Lord, because He is good, and His mercies endure forever. Yea, let them which have been redeemed of the Lord, shew how He hath delivered them from the hand of the oppressor. When they wandered in the; desert wilderness out of the way, and found no city to dwell in, both hungry, and thirsty, their soul was overwhelmed in them. Let them confess before the Lord His loving kindness, and His wonderful works before the sons of men.[2]

The fact is that the Pilgrims are granted original status. They are considered ground zero. American literature is thus shaped as a celebration of their courage. They escaped bigotry, injustice, and religious intolerance.

---

[2] William Bradford, *Of Plymouth Plantation*, edited by Harold Paget (New York: Portculis Books, 2016). The literature of the British settlers has less of an aesthetic value than a historical purpose. It wasn't written with the generate aesthetic responses in readers; instead, its objective was to chronicle the trials and tribulations of the colonial enterprise.

As it unfolds, American literature will depend on wistfulness. How to survey the house, the land, built by these champions of liberty? For successive generations, that languor will stress the promise of conviviality: *e pluribus unum*. For the American quest is, at its core, utopian, a word that in Greek means "there is no such place." The nation's literature is thus about finding cohesion at any cost: the allusive, elusive, and illusive *we*.

The mission is the heart of Robert Frost's "The Gift Outright" (1941), arguably one of the most important poems in the American literary canon. Frost read publicly at President John F. Kennedy's inauguration. The poet states that the American land, Massachusetts and Virginia and other places, was American before there were Americans, when "we were England's, still colonials,/ Possessing what we still were unpossessed by,/ Possessed by what we now no more possessed."[3]

The communion between land and inhabitants is natural: possessed by it and possessed in it, America waits for a call. It is part of the nineteenth-century doctrine of Manifest Destiny, built on the conviction that American institutions, inherently virtuous, are called to redeem whatever they come across in their westward expansionist quest in order to make it make it resemble the image of those in the east. The term was coined in 1845 by newspaper editor John O'Sullivan, who promoted the annexation of Texas and the Oregon Country, but is easily dated back to figures like Thomas Paine, who in his pamphlet *Common Sense* (1776) argued that America was about building the world again in a way that hadn't been done since Noah. This destiny is essential and

[3] Robert Frost, "The Gift Outright," *The Poetry of Robert Frost* (New York: Henry Holt, 1969). The poem strikes me as an example of Manifest Destiny. The territorial claim it makes has a biblical undertone.

implacable, not led by human conviction but by divine certainty. Putting it bluntly, the mission is to build as large a Garden of Eden because big is better than small. Big is powerful.

America expects devotion because it is ready to devote itself to those who join her, as long as they are ready not to withhold themselves, to commit their fullness "from salvation to surrender."

It is all about sacrifice. The land requires full devotion. It demands that its inhabitants surrender themselves to fate. There will be a price to pay. In the land is also its history: the wars it will engage in, its colonial quests, its abuses of power have a single objective: to bring happiness to its citizens. "Such as we were we gave ourselves outright," Frost continues. Behind that Manifest Destiny is the conviction that the Almighty is the driving force in national affairs, that God wants America to realize its own purpose.

Since the starts, the country has both embraced and rejected religious dogma. The Pilgrims were running away from it, only to embrace a different modality once they settled across the Atlantic. That duality between belief and secularism, which might be seen in old times in the debate on birth control and is tangible in the disputes over abortion, LGBTQ rights, and other morally polarizing issues, is proof of the degree to which religion matters.

Indeed, it is often said that in America progress is the outcome of secular conceptions, that science and technology only advance at the speed they do thanks to the conviction that God isn't actually in control of the universe, and that God, as Albert Einstein stated, is an explainable force that "does not play dice with the universe."[4] This from a man who professed not to believe in a

---

[4] Einstein wrote this line in 1945 in a letter to Cal Tech theoretical physicist Paul Epstein. The question of change in the divine design is the focus of long-standing philosophical inquiries. American philosopher William James, brother

personal God yet appreciated religion as a source of morality and an organizer of social structures.

Truth is, America is a deeply devout country. Portions of it—the Bible Belt, for instance—verge on fundamentalism. Its founding documents, from the U.S. constitution to the Pledge of Alliance, make clear the role the Almighty plays in the shaping of the nation. God blesses America as a nation. God also blessed the people of the United States.

American literature might be read as an exploration of this blessing. Bradford and other British settlers justified their mission as a biblical mandate: they were sent across the Atlantic in search of a New Canaan. In the Jacksonian era, Alexis de Tocqueville, a French visitor to the United States on an assignment to write about the prison system who in the end produced a book of infinite wonder, *Democracy in America* (1835), was mesmerized by the fact that religion and democracy worked hand in hand, something impossible in France. The basis, in his view, was the conception, later ratified into law, that people, in order to practice their own faith, needed to respect that of others.

That mutual approach gave room to a marketplace of faiths and to the conviction that every one supported its own view of the divine. Obviously, Christianity, as the original religion of the European settlers, and the bible as its sacred text, was seen as holding a special case.

To this day, American writers wrestle with this view. Some, like Edmund Wilson, the patrician literary critic who authored *Axel's Castle: A Study of the Imaginative Literature of 1870–1930* (1931) and for

of novelist Henry James, wrote that "all our scientific and philosophic ideas are altars of unknown gods" (Lecture at Harvard Divinity School, March 13, 1884).

years wrote for the *New Yorker* magazine, argued that "we must simply live without religion."[5] But in America many more look at faith, and at God in particular, as central to the national character, an orchestrator of social affairs who grants meaning to every action, individual and collective.

Ralph Waldo Emerson, one of the New England transcendentalists, viewed God not as a promoter of Christianity—he was averse to organized religion, believing, as he stated in his journals, that "God build his temple in the heart, on the ruins of churches & religions"—but as a supreme intellectual being, in Spinoza's sense of the term, who ruled the universe through beauty and order. In his essay "Nature," Emerson wrote:

> Standing on the bare ground,—my head bathed by the blithe air and uplifted into infinite space,—all mean egotism vanishes. I become a transparent eyeball; I am nothing; I see all; the currents of the Universal Being circulate through me; I am part or parcel of God.[6]

Although in his book *Representative Men* (1850) Emerson didn't include Jesus—the six essays featured are on Plato, Swedenborg, Montaigne, Shakespeare, Napoleon, and Goethe—he wrote about him reverently, as a leader guided by internal clarity. He plays a major role in "On Self-Reliance" (1841):

> Is it so bad then to be misunderstood? Pythagoras was misunderstood, and Socrates, and Jesus, and Luther, and Copernicus, and

---

[5] Edmund Wilson, *Literary Essays and Reviews of the 1920s and 30s: The Shores of Light / Axel's Castle / Uncollected Reviews*, edited by Lewis M. Dabney (New York: Library of America, 2007).

[6] This and the previous quotes come from Ralph Waldo Emerson, "Nature," *Essays and Lectures: Nature: Addresses and Lectures, Essays: First and Second Series, Representative Men/English Traits, The Conduct of Life* (New York: Library of America, 1983).

Galileo, and Newton, and every pure and wise spirit that ever took flesh. To be great is to be misunderstood.

Atheism is the religion of reason. Whitman thought that "God is a mean-spirited, pugnacious bully bent on revenge against His children for failing to live up to his impossible standards." (Ironically, he wrote "His" with an upper case H.)

He believed that "pointing to another world will never stop vice among us; shedding light over this world can alone help us." And he argued: "I like the scientific spirit—the holding off, the being sure but not too sure, the willingness to surrender ideas when the evidence is against them: this is ultimately fine—it always keeps the way beyond open."

All these are white male authors. While they have taken control of the debate, it is ludicrous to think they own it. In fact, in American literature feminine explorations of the divine are often more inspired, if nothing else because of the subaltern role women have played in the nation's history. They have been the ones who, lighting the domestic torch, have had intimate conversations with the Almighty.

For instance, in Flannery O'Connor, in *Wise Blood* (1952), which looks at religious fanaticism as an extreme psychological behavior, the message is that America is a nation of religious rabble-rousers. Since O'Connor's universe is the South, that conviction emerges from its destitute, racially fractured social texture.

That fracture is also at the heart of Alice Walker's *The Color Purple* (1982), which offers a direct view of religiosity among Blacks in rural Georgia in the nineteen-hundreds. Structured as an epistolary novel, its protagonist, Celie, is a 14-year-old uneducated woman who is a descendant of slaves. Her life of extreme poverty and sexual abuse are explored in minute detail. She writes her letters to God. In that sense, the novel is an act of devotion to God, just as is offered almost ubiquitously in America.

Yes, God leads America by the hand, pushing it forward, either out of knowledge or ignorance.

And America is never static. She exists in a permanent state of mutation. It might just be a superficial type of change, a change in appearances, for its essence must remain intact for future generations to have a share in the quest the Pilgrims started, as is clear at the outset of the quixotic Declaration of Independence (approved July 4, 1776), that "it is a truth self-evident that all people are created equal" regardless of their race, religion, and ideology, that "they are endowed with certain unalienable rights," and "that among these rights are life, liberty and the pursuit of happiness."

It is a promise postponed, a promised betrayal. Yet its insistence, by sheer repetition, turns it into a mantra: America is an experiment where people are happy becoming who they are. That's the AMERICAN DREAM, spelled with capitals and capitalized as a social, economic, and psychological incentive. Have the courage to be yourself.

The German Dream? The Mexican Dream? The Chinese Dream? No other nations have a similar behaviorist mechanism. Not that they are, for all intents and purposes, dreamless. But in them dreams aren't national; they are strictly personal.[7] In

---

[7] On average, a healthy person spends approximately a third, maybe a fourth of life asleep. And sleep, lest we need to be reminded, is not exactly the opposite of activity. We don't just relax when we're asleep; our minds are actively engaged, processing emotions and information. We dream while we're asleep, even if we don't always remember a dream's content.

I never cease to be puzzled by the disregard we have in contemporary culture—by which I mean this all-confining modern Western civilization of

ours—toward our dreams. Occasionally I sit in a coffee shop next to a stranger who is casually describing what sounds like a meaningful dream; but the conversation quickly switches gear, as if narrating a dream were nothing more than a palate cleanser.

I love to dream but I seldom remember my dreams. And when I do, the moment I attempt to narrate what I saw in the theater of my mind I feel like a falsifier: words aren't sufficient tools to express their complexity. Throughout my life I have had a few dreams that recycle themselves: same content, different format.

Describing dreams is one thing, interpreting them is another. I dislike the temptation to analyze dreams. Sigmund Freud made a name out of it. For him, dreams are manifestations of our unconscious, garbled thoughts waiting to be deciphered. They mostly showcase sexual desires we don't allow ourselves to recognize in rational terms. That approach to me is nonsense, even more so than the illogical nature of dreams.

Dreams are much more: they are drives toward freedom; they are expressions of spiritual longing; they are reconfigurations of the self. Through dreams we take vacations from rationality, which is often mercilessly judgmental.

It would be delightful if we could borrow another person's dream, even if only once. I would love to dream Shakespeare's dreams, for I admire no one more.

As for nightmares, I'm struck by the word in English we use to describe them: the she-horse of night. (Needless to say, this isn't in every language: the word in Spanish is *pesadilla*; in German, *albtraum*; in Italian, *incubo*.) In Henry Fuseli's famous painting "The Nightmare" (1781), a white horse with flashy eyes makes an appearance through a curtain while a voluptuous woman, with an incubus crouched on her chest, sleeps. The message is clear: in nightmares, we are at the mercy of demons.

Another version—not only of nightmares—is that, as, as W. B. Yeats believed, "in dreams begins responsibility." We find resources while we sleep. And we achieve clarity. I myself often choose to "consult with the pillow," as the folk saying goes, before I make a crucial decision.

In Sufism, the whole universe is perceived to be God's dream. The moment God wakes up, everything vanishes irrevocably. We must, for that reason, keep God dreaming; it's the only way to perpetuate ourselves. And in a particularly resonant part of the *Sefer ha-Zohar*, the most important book in Jewish mysticism, which is prone to labyrinthine structures, God also dreams Itself.

In Mexico, dreams are conduits to communicate with the dead. In part, that is what *Día de los Muertos* is about. The deceased are still with us, in invisible form. They guide us and advise us, mostly through dreams and spiritual communication.

In Phoenicia and Mesopotamia, dreams were seen as prophetic—that is, they foresaw the future. That quality is present in ancient traditions, from the *Iliad* to

America, instead, dreams are cooperative enterprises. Although they are performed individually, their influence is enormous in the social network.

Your American Dream is as important as mine because if you succeed, I succeed as well. That's how neighborhoods are built—when your home is next to mine, independent yet interrelated.

Even American counter-narratives like those offered by the Beat Generation—William S. Burroughs, Allen Ginsberg, and Jack Kerouac, among others—in rejecting the status quo are always propelled by their own version of the American Dream. In *On the Road* (1957), Kerouac states:

the *Popol Vuh*, and, of course the bible. Samuel, Ezekiel, and other biblical prophets have an active dream life. Maimonides, the medieval Spanish philosopher, believed dreams to be the channel through which the Almighty communicates with the prophets. In the *Guide for the Perplexed* (1190), he postulated Moses not only as the prophet of prophets but the dreamer of dreamers.

Some of the best passages in modern literature are about dreams: Don Quixote in the Cave of Montesinos, Alice lost in Wonderland, Pascal's dreams, Gregor Samsa waking up after uneasy dreams to discover he had become a huge bug, the town of Macondo in *One Hundred Years of Solitude* suffering an epidemic of insomnia.

Does the syntax of our language define how we dream? And are the dreams of childhood like the dreams of adulthood or should they be categorized differently? In the years before her death, my mother-in-law told me that her dreams were now mostly populated with people she had never seen.

Are dreams inevitably in the present tense? Is there a past or a future tense inside a dream, any dream? Likewise, I never see myself in my own dreams, yet I know the point of view in the dream is mine. Can our dreams be narrated by someone else? Can they be in the third person?

It is no doubt significant that we use the same word, dream, to describe what we see while we are asleep and what we hope for. Perhaps it's because the future is in itself a dream. Rev. Martin Luther King, Jr.'s "I Have a Dream" speech has therefore two meanings: the ideological and the oneiric.

I conclude—how else?—with Shakespeare's last full play, *The Tempest* (1611), Act 4, Scene 1: "We are such *stuff/* As *dreams* are *made* on; and our little *life/* Is rounded with a sleep."

Our little life, indeed.

I believed in a good home, in sane and sound living, in good food, good times, work, faith and hope. I have always believed in these things. It was with some amazement that I realized I was one of the few people in the world who really believed in these things without going around making a dull middle class philosophy out of it. I was suddenly left with nothing in my hands but a handful of crazy stars.[8]

Those crazy starts are the currency needed for Americans to constantly refashion themselves.

2. Native Trail

Obviously, the concept of Manifest Destiny is just a convenient truth told, like any other socially constructed truth, to justify a *Weltanschauung*.

The Pilgrims, Frost forgot to mention, weren't the first in the land. It was the aboriginals. And Viking fleets led by Eric the Red and others. And Spanish explorers, conquistadors, and missionaries like Pánfilo de Narváez, Álvar Núñez Cabeza de Vaca, Juan de Oñate, Eusebio Kino, and Marcos de Niza. And French colonizers such as Robert Cavelier de La Salle and Pierre La Moyne d'Iberville.

Few other countries are as conflicted about nativism as America is. Falsely conflicted, for at the beginning there was an aboriginal population. Yet that population was ignored, pushed aside, silenced. Americans make a conscious effort to

---

[8] Jack Kerouac, *On the Road* (New York: Viking, 1956). Disdainful of Kerouac's style, Truman Capote famously said that he didn't write, he merely typed. Yet that liberating attitude—linked to what Surrealist poet and essayist Andre Breton called "automatic writing," has found countless followers in America, a country that sees literature as a therapeutic tool.

know—nothing!—about it. Other than as a source of guilt, the natives don't count.

There is no magisterial *Popol Vuh* of the Maya K'iche', a prodigious book of origins that chronicles the beginning of the world, the deities that control the underworld called Xibalba, and the plight of survival during the conquest. In part, this absence is due to the sparseness of the indigenous landscape in what is today the United States, from the Shawnee in Oklahoma to the Caushatta in Louisiana to the Passamaquoddy in Maine.

Unlike Mesoamérica, for instance, where the Aztecs, Maya, and other civilizations reigned as the Spaniards made their way, or in Peru, defined by the Inca, the tribes encountered by the Pilgrims were small.

The wave of early Native American writing starts in the nineteenth century: William Apess's *A Son of the Forest* (1829) and George Copway's *The Life, History, and Travels of Kah-ge-ga-gahbowh* (1847). These are stories of conversion to Christianity, though. They coincide, and respond to the popularity of, mainstream narratives like James Fenimore Cooper's *The Last of the Mohicans* (1826), Catharine Maria Sedgwick's *Hope Leslie* (1827), and Henry Wadsworth Longfellow's *Song of Hiawatha* (1855), in which "Indians" are de facto depicted as barbarous.

Before that, there are folktales and other forms of oral tradition from the Cherokee, Cheyenne, Iroquois, Navajo, Osage, Sioux, and other. But they are seen as childish: unformed, unprocessed, and, therefore, inconsequential.

Only after the Civil Rights era, at the end of the sixties, when America became less homogenized, more multiethnic, was there more room allocated—long promised yet far from enough—to the native's voice. In her poem "An American Sunrise" (2019), Joy

Harjo, a member of the Muscogee (Creek) Nation and a U.S. Poet Laureate who came of age after the Civil Rights struggle, wrote about the journey to return to the source of her ancestors to reclaim her voice as well as the sovereignty and the humanity of her people.

In it, Harjo talks about running out of breath: "We were running out of breath, as we ran out to meet ourselves." Sin and the devil, she states, are Christian inventions designed to generate guilt. The indigenous population was undermined, pushed down. It was abused, exiled from its own land onto reservations that functioned as de facto concentration camps, left in limbo—without justice, without a sense of self. Yet "We are still America," in spite of "the rumors of our demise."[9]

Harjo's affirmation is an embrace of roots: even through rejection, her people are very much part of that unfinished collective project, that call to congregate around a utopian idea. In fact, for a nation in which the past is always up for grabs it is stunning the degree to which the dead matter in America. They don't just rest in peace in their graves; their presence among the living is constant, particularly when it comes to nativism. Who is and who isn't an authentic American is often resolved by pointing to one's ancestry.

This is not to say that the country looks at death straight in the eye. Proof of it is the abysmal difference between say *Día de los Muertos* and Halloween. In Mexico, the former is seen as a holiday of communal engagement. From October 31 to November 2, people not only picnic in graveyards near the colorfully decorated tombs of their loved ones who have departed this world; they

---

[9] Joy Harjo, *An American Sunrise: Poems* (New York: W. W. Norton, 2019).

also sleep over, playing music, singing, and drinking. Those dead are said to join them in merriment, establishing a dialogue that extends beyond the holiday. They protect their living relatives, they offer council, they accompany them in their existential path. In other words, the cemetery isn't a site of fright.[10]

Halloween is the just the opposite: a marketing parade that makes fun of the dead. Masks, customs, loads of makeup featuring wounds, blood, and other props—the objective is simple: to ridicule, to deride, to mock. Not one's dead relatives; they would never be part of the charade. The targets are rather anonymous: Frankenstein, Dracula, the sitting president, and whoever is misbehaving as Speaker of the House. This pagan holiday has nothing to do with sacredness; its whole purpose is to allow people to be as outrageous—as profane—as they might desire to be during a single day.

Still, the dead in America do speak, albeit in different ways: through monuments, mausoleums, and memorials. All nations build these sites, and on occasion, as a result of recrimination, reconsider them, to the point of even taking them down, as the Black Lives Matter movement has. In other words, sites of memory are sacred until they become profane. The difference is that America, more than other countries, is fixated upon the future, which makes it approach the past as merely a steppingstone. For as frantic as the nation is about moving forward, as it often claims to do, is it also about turning the past into stone. Parks, avenues,

---

[10] First published in book form in 1950, Octavio Paz's *The Labyrinth of Solitude: Life and Thought in Mexico* (New York: Grove, 1962, translated by Lysander Kemp) explores, eloquently through a psycho-historical prism, this national relationship with death. The first chapter is about the Pachucos, Mexican-Americans living in Los Angeles in the mid-twentieth century whom Paz sees as excessive, a deviation of the Mexican norm.

schools, community centers are named after, and filled with effigies of, luminaries of yesteryear. While they might not have acted as saints, they are turned into icons.

On occasion, in a battle cry for change these statues are brought down, as is the case of a slew of Confederate generals. The same happens with literary classics that might have been enshrined yet no longer speak to new readers. Take the case of Harriet Beecher Stowe's *Uncle Tom's Cabin* (1852). This is the novel that ignited the American Civil War and maybe also the novel that decided it. In its ferocious anti-slavery position, it argued for the humanity of slaves. Yet its rhetoric has fallen into misuse.

That it was written by a proto-suffragist and a woman is symptomatic of its strength. The American constitution was made by white male slave-owners. Upon meeting Stowe, Abraham Lincoln purportedly said: "So this is the little lady who started this great war." But in wanting to spread good will, *Uncle Tom's Cabin*— starting with its subtitle, "Life among the Lowly"—tarnished it.

While other books of the time have survived, its depictions of Blacks, "mulattos" (those of mixed ancestry that includes white European and Black African roots), "sambos" (from the Spanish *zambo*, in reference to a person of mixed African and indigenous descent), "quadroon" (one-quarter African and three-quarters European), "octoroon" (from the Latin *octo-*, one-eighth Black), and "hexadecaroon" (one-sixteenth Black) are offensive. The response is to "shelf" it, to bury it in ignominy. Stowe's novel never disappears; it just exists in a limbo of eternal disdain, regardless of its function in antebellum America.

Also in regard to how Americans dialogue with the past, consider Faulkner's novel *As I Lay Dying* (1930). Known as a prime example of "Southern Gothic," it is narrated by dozens of characters collectively involved in burying, physically and metaphorically, the corpse of the family matriarch, Addie Bundren, in Jefferson, Mississippi. The journey from her deathbed to the hole that will be her ultimate home is full of obstacles. The family members are a bunch of misfits. Their conflicting stories clash with one another. The novel's title comes from Book XI of Homer's *Odyssey*, in which Agamemnon tells Odysseus: "As I lay dying, the woman with the dog's eyes would not close my eyes as I descended into Hades."[11]

Faulkner knows that to bury one's dead is an act of closure. Those before us will precede us to the grave. It is part of the game. But burial is also about expiation. To bury the dead is to travel to an imaginary world where memory is the only way to relate to one's ancestors. They are in our minds, in our hearts. They are no longer who they once were; instead, they have become our fictions. They are imprisoned in our fantasy the way we ourselves will be imprisoned in the fantasy of our successors.

The novel was written over a period of six weeks, methodically every night from midnight to 4 a.m. Faulkner purportedly didn't change a single word before it reached the press. Addie Bundren's funeral procession is a charade. The misunderstandings among her descendants are intense. They are unworthy of her. The act of laying her under the ground is a comedy of manners. Is this what the living do with the dead?

Once the ground receives the departed, it becomes sacred. Indeed, the foundation of civilization is the cemetery. It is a holy ground. Its meaning is clear: our flesh is in this soil, our blood, our dreams. The cemetery makes the land ours in metaphysical ways.

---

[11] Homer, *Odyssey*. Translated by William Marris (London: Oxford University Press, 1925).

It rebuilds the umbilical cord cut at birth. This is where we belong because this where our ancestors lie buried.

Turning suffering into words, death into memory, is the task of literature. But, as Faulkner shows, words are always clumsy, inefficient. No matter what we do, they come short. Not only because they can't apprehend reality but because American reality itself is clumsy, inefficient. To allow Addie Bundren's corpse to finally rest, the living would need to be at peace. Yet peace is elusive among the living. They are always in a state of flight, on the run, looking for another adventure, for a way to manifest their individuality anew.

And there is another way to commune with the dead in American literature: through translation. While I shall talk about this topic in Chapter IV, "Surviving Democracy," at this point it makes sense to explore an example.

From the mid-eighteenth century onward, translation was a strategy to appreciate the scope of Europe's universalist goals. Goethe's concept of *Weltliteratur*, in a diary entry dated January 31, 1827, is therefore "Occidentalist," e.g., west-driven. It envisioned literature as expanding from Europe into the larger world.[12] For a variety of reasons, almost since the birth of America the nation has made a commitment toward recycling the classics in American English. Ovid's *Metamorphoses*, the *Analects* of Confucius, the

---

[12] See Edward Said's book *Orientalism* (New York: Pantheon, 1978) and *Occidentalism: The West in the Eyes of Its Enemies* (London: Atlantic Books, 2004) by Ian Buruma and Avishai Margalit. I spent a couple of afternoons with Said in the late eighties, when he visited the wife of his friend Eqbal Ahmad, who was my Upper West Side neighbor. Anyway, translation always has a locus, which is where the translator sits culturally in the act of rendering a text unforeign. Thought-provoking reading on this theme is David Damrosch's *What Is World Literature?* (Princeton: Princeton University Press, 2003) and Mads Thomsen's *Mapping World Literature* (New York: Continuum, 2008).

Icelandic sagas, *La chanson de Roland*, Flaubert's *Madame Bovary* ....
It is crucial to remember the extent to which translation is an act
of recovery. What is translated into English is also remembered
because English is the tool of memory.

Among my favorite is Henry Wadsworth Longfellow's version
of Dante's *Inferno* (1867):

> Midway upon the journey of our life
> I found myself within a forest dark,
> For the straightforward pathway had been lost.
> Ah me! how hard a thing it is to say
> What was this forest savage, rough, and stern,
> Which in the very thought renews the fear.
> So bitter is it, death is little more;
> But of the good to treat, which there I found,
> Speak will I of the other things I saw there.
> I cannot well repeat how there I entered,
> So full was I of slumber at the moment
> In which I had abandoned the true way.[13]

A couple of years after the American Civil War finally came to a
close, Longfellow, through Dante's pilgrimage led by Virgil and
in search of his beloved Beatrice, enabled the readers of a deeply
Christian country mourning the deaths of their husbands and
sons, to participate in a national séance session to converse with
the spirits while exploring the underworld.

The translation came out three years after the death of
Longfellow's own wife, Frances Appleton, who died in an accident

---

[13] Dante Alighieri, *The Divine Comedy*, translated by Henry Wadsworth
Longfellow (Boston: Appleton, 1867). In unrhymed terzines, Longfellow's rendition was the first to make the entire sequence of *Inferno*, *Purgatory*, and *Paradiso*
available to English-language readers. The interest it generated still reverberates
in current generations.

when her dress caught on fire. The tragedy devastated Longfellow; he never fully recovered from it. He himself was also searching for spiritual comfort.

To prepare his *Divine Comedy*, every Wednesday starting in 1864 he—on the faculty at Harvard—would invite his friends, including Charles Eliot Norton, James Russell Lowell, and William Dean Howells, to come over. His three-volume publication was hugely successful.

Translation is more than simply dressing up a book in new clothes. It is a repositioning of that book for a new generation. In this respect, Anna Brickhouse, in *The Unsettlement of America* (2015), is right in inviting audiences to go beyond the easy either/or of literature framed in its own time and place. By looking at a "more nuanced and capacious understanding of the practices and politics of translation, one that resists the understandable scholarly tendency to apprehend translation in the early modern era largely as a tool of empire, a dutiful metonymy of *translatio imperii*," it is possible to appreciate how a translation serves the immediate needs of its readers.

That is, it not only matters what the original says but in what way the translation comes alive again. And so do the dead.

In any case, in America the conversation with the dead is a matter of capital. People come from somewhere. That provenance grants them cultural cache. Italians safeguard Italianness, Irish Irishness, Blacks Blackness, Jews Jewishness, and so on. That is ethnic neighborhoods are about: an anchoring site. The same goes for ethnic holidays (St. Patrick's Day) and day parades (Puerto Rican Day Parade, etc.).

Conversely, this rooting allows Americans to boast about their global reach. Everyone has relatives in another land. Everyone's family is worldly, their holiday table a culinary feast of traditional flavors from places as disparate as China, Mexico, Norway, Rwanda, and Vietnam. To be tied to the land where one's family immigrated from is to boast about one's collective memory.

Needless to say, in a nation where memory is frighteningly short, that is an asset worth protecting. If nothing else, it exercises the imagination. Americans love to be nostalgic of the journey done by previous generations. They dream of it as a voyage from and to Arcadia: treacherous, unstable, full of surprises yet astonishingly rewarding. Every immigrant trek ends up being from rags to riches. A fanciful new home awaits the travel around the corner.

3. Original Sin

In an 1863 proclamation that advocated a national day of fasting, Abraham Lincoln said it behooves the American people "to humble ourselves before the offended Power, to confess our national sins, and to pray for clemency and forgiveness."

America's original sin is slavery. Blacks were bought as chattel slaves. They were dehumanized, corralled, brought in chains. In part, this had to do with the lower indigenous population. In Latin America, that native population was enslaved by the Spanish and Portuguese imperial forces. Ironically, it wasn't until figures like Fray Bartolomé de Las Casas, known as "the defender of the Indians," orchestrated a global campaign to call attention to the European abuses of the natives in the Caribbean Basin and elsewhere that an alternative policy took shape. That policy involved the transportation of millions of African slaves.

Eager to build a strong economy in the Thirteen Colonies, the English settlers also needed labor. But the Indians in those regions were few and bellicose. The response was the investment in the Middle Passage: the journey of Blacks as indentured species from Africa to the Americas. In the United States, 12.5 million people were transacted upon. Around 15 percent died *en route*.

There is no escaping it: the foundation of America was built on the shameless commerce of humans. The Founding Fathers and Mothers—George and Martha Washington, Thomas Jefferson, James Madison, John Jay, and others—were slave-owners.

Slave narratives populate American literature from the eighteenth century onward. They are a reminder of the misery of slavery. So does slave poetry. Phillis Wheatley is an eloquent example. This is her poem "On Being Brought from Africa to America," where the biblical resonances can't be clearer:

> 'Twas mercy brought me from my *Pagan* land,
> Taught my benighted soul to understand
> That there's a God, that there's a *Saviour* too:
> Once I redemption neither sought nor knew.
> Some view our sable race with scornful eye,
> "Their colour is a diabolic die."
> Remember, *Christians*, *Negros*, black as *Cain*,
> May be refin'd, and join th' angelic train.[14]

In his seminal collection of essays *The Souls of Black Folks* (1903), Black intellectual W. E. B. Du Bois writes about the echoes of bondage:

---

[14] Phillis Wheatley, "On Being Brought from Africa to America," *Becoming Americans: Four Centuries of Immigrant Writing*, edited by Ilan Stavans (New York: Library of America, 2011).

Between me and the other world there is ever an unasked question: unasked by some through feelings of delicacy; by others through the difficulty of rightly framing it. All, nevertheless, flutter round it. They approach me in a half-hesitant sort of way, eye me curiously or compassionately, and then, instead of saying directly, How does it feel to be a problem? they say, I know an excellent colored man in my town; or, I fought at Mechanicsville; or, Do not these Southern outrages make your blood boil? At these I smile, or am interested, or reduce the boiling to a simmer, as the occasion may require. To the real question, How does it feel to be a problem? I answer seldom a word.

Du Bois's answer is an exploration of the unacknowledged suffering, the "double-consciousness" that results from being, at once and forever, insider and outsider. However, the problem of the twentieth century, he states ominously (his book is almost concurrent with Joseph Conrad's *Heart of Darkness* [1899], about the European colonial venture in Africa), "is the problem of the color line."

The history of the American Negro is the history of this strife,— this longing to attain self-conscious manhood, to merge his double self into a better and truer self. In this merging he wishes neither of the older selves to be lost. He would not Africanize America, for America has too much to teach the world and Africa. He would not bleach his Negro soul in a flood of white Americanism, for he knows that Negro blood has a message for the world. He simply wishes to make it possible for a man to be both a Negro and an American, without being cursed and spit upon by his fellows, without having the doors of Opportunity closed roughly in his face.[15]

[15] W. E. B. Du Bois, *Writings: The Suppression of the African Slave Trade / The Souls of Black Folk / Dust of Dawn / Essays and Articles* (New York: The Library of America, 1987).

The wound of the original sin doesn't heal. It is infected, endlessly saturating pus. The quests for change are unavoidable reminders of an ongoing subjugation: the assimilationist views of Booker T. Washington, advocated to Du Bois's chagrin; the epic stance of Rosa Parks; and the Rev. Martin Luther King, Jr.'s "Letter from Birmingham Jail" (1963), with the aching line "Perhaps I have once again been too optimistic" making it clear that the path forward is planted with suffering, and his "I Have a Dream" speech in Washington, D.C., on August 28, 1963, in which he prophetically is visited by a dream in which his four little children will one day live in a nation "where they will not be judged by the color of their skin but by the content of their character."

The wound of the original sin doesn't heal. Shamefully, America keeps procrastinating its readiness to reject the painful past. During Reconstruction, Blacks, already free, were ghettoized in the South, their chances of a better future for themselves and their children curtailed by negligible educational and economic incentives. The result was the construction of a working class built on new forms of dehumanization.

The central metaphor in Ralph Ellison's novel *Invisible Man* (1952) couldn't be more appropriate, clear in the opening lines:

> I am an invisible man. No I am not a spook like those who haunted Edgar Allen Poe; nor am I one of your Hollywood movie ectoplasms. I am a man of substance, of flesh and bone, fiber and liquids, and I might even be said to possess a mind. I am invisible, simply because people refuse to see me.[16]

---

[16] Ralph Ellison, *Invisible Man* (New York: Random House, 1952).

Ellison indicts American culture: Blacks exist, yes, but only as ghosts. His narrative impugns the need for people to open their eyes, to see the racism that is palpable everywhere.

This is clear from the invectives by other members of the Harlem Renaissance, such as Zora Neale Hurston, whose novel *Their Eyes Were Watching God* (1937) explores gender roles in a lucid, jazzy language, and Nella Larsen's novella *Passing* (1929), whose characters are caught in the neither-here-nor-there of Black and white cultures.

These literary explorations are a record of the nation's raw memory. Yes, books keep the evidence so readers might find it tomorrow. In *Giovanni's Room* (1956), James Baldwin, one of the most eloquent, clear-headed twentieth-century American writers, explains how it all came down to him, by just walking around on the street, by just reading books: "You think your pain and your heartbreak are unprecedented in the history of the world, but then you read. It was books that taught me that the things that tormented me most were the very things that connected me with all the people who were alive, who had ever been alive."[17]

At some point, America is fated to undergo, yet again, a deliverance, its history of Black degradation a bomb that will explode in people's faces. The Civil Rights era was an advance of such a reckoning, as is the Black Lives Matter movement. For the weight of slavery isn't only imprinted in the memory of the oppressed. It is also ciphered in the victimizer's forehead: I brutalized you, it states, turning you into my beast of burden. As a result, *I* will forever live in infamy.

[17] James Baldwin, *Giovanni's Room* (New York: Dial Press, 1956).

4. "Give Me Your Tired"

In terms of immigration, Emma Lazarus's sonnet "The New Colossus" (1883) is ground zero of American literature. An auspicious, emblematic, and ultimately transformative poem, at once an aesthetic appreciation of strangers and a declaration of national purpose, it is engraved in the pedestal of the Statue of Liberty; it greeted newcomers upon arriving to "the sea-washed, sunset gates" of New York City and, by synecdoche, the United States. Lady Liberty, with pomp, welcomed them to the "air-bridged harbor." That she does it in English, not in the languages of immigration, whichever they might be, is in itself a statement. Come to me, she says. I will give you shelter. I will also give you a place. I will give you a self.

Lazarus, a Sephardic Jew with knowledge of German (she translated into English Heinrich Heine and also a handful of medieval Hebrew poets like Yehuda Halevi and Shlomo ibn Gabirol that Heine had rendered into his own language) and an activist involved in supporting the arrival of Italian, Polish, Russian, and some Ottoman immigrants to the United States, understood the vigor of democracy.

She realized it was the contract that democracy offers—equality, liberty, and justice for all—that was a lightning rod everywhere on the globe. More than a century after independence and decades after a disastrous civil war, America was a beacon. Yet it didn't want to be alone, isolated, disengaged. It found its strength in the need to welcome those in search for a new beginning. She saw the nation not as a place but as an idea. The eloquent last two stanzas of the sonnet read:

Not like the brazen giant of Greek fame,
With conquering limbs astride from land to land;
Here at our sea-washed, sunset gates shall stand
A mighty woman with a torch, whose flame
Is the imprisoned lightning, and her name
Mother of Exiles. From her beacon-hand
Glows world-wide welcome; her mild eyes command
The air-bridged harbor that twin cities frame.
"Keep, ancient lands, your storied pomp!" cries she
With silent lips. "Give me your tired, your poor,
Your huddled masses yearning to breathe free,
The wretched refuse of your teeming shore.
Send these, the homeless, tempest-tost to me,
I lift my lamp beside the golden door!"[18]

That welcoming is, in and of itself, a dictum: I receive you, Lady
Liberty announces, since you've made a journey in order to be
received. The agreement is verbal. You must understand these
words crafted into a sonnet, you must read them aloud to your
children and your children's children. You must bow to them. You
must also live by them. That's the mantra. Literature is a contract:
it recognizes a bond, a pact, a convention.

The process of assimilation won't be easy. Everyone arrives to
America as if into a new planet. But each planet has its own metabolism: to live in it, one must start from scratch. Among all planets,
this promises to be one in an eternal state of renewal. That's clear
from its place in the geography of the world's imagination: the
New World. The Old World is old, exhausted, in decay. It is intol-
erant to originality. But here things are different. You will have a
new start, a start that will happen as a series of challenges. There

---

[18] Emma Lazarus, *Selected Poems*, edited by Esther Schor (New York: Library of
America, 2005).

will need to be a refamiliarization with reality as a whole: the taste of food, the cadence of the language, the way people walk, how they dress, the language they speak. There will be a reeducation. What else is the reinvention of the past if not that?

Yet after it, America will be *yours*, with whatever origins you want as roots. It will be yours in a way the Old World never allowed. As long as you're entrepreneurial, as long as you're individualistic, as long as you partake in the dream that is America, you will have a share of it.

Emblematically, even while her age was defined by immigration, Lazarus refers to newcomers as exiles. America loves to give different names to those who arrive: settlers, pilgrims, slaves, exiles, refugees, immigrants, expats, visitors, tourists .... Each of these terms carries a different connotation. In "The New Colossus," those exiles arriving, according to *Merriam-Webster*, are in "the state or a period of forced absence from one's country or home."

They were expelled from their "ancient lands." Refugees might also arrive in similar conditions, "fleeing to a foreign country or power to escape danger or persecution." But immigrants don't do the journey out of compulsion, unless that compulsion is understood to be personal. An immigrant is "a person who comes up to a country to take up permanent residence." The effort is premeditated; it is also driven by individual reasons.

Lazarus's poem champions immigrants as self-determined heroes. They will renew the nation, infusing it with fresh energy. They will be the ones carrying on the dream, allowing future immigrants to come in as well.

Interestingly, the poet didn't come up suddenly with the conviction to command world-wide welcome. Shortly before "The

New Colossus," she wrote another sonnet with a similar theme. It is called "1492" (1883):

> Thou two-faced year, Mother of Change and Fate,
> Didst weep when Spain cast forth with flaming sword,
> The children of the prophets of the Lord,
> Prince, priest, and people, spurned by zealot hate.
> Hounded from sea to sea, from state to state,
> The West refused them, and the East abhorred.
> No anchorage the known world could afford,
> Close-locked was every port, barred every gate.
> Then smiling, thou unveil'dst, O two-faced year,
> A virgin world where doors of sunset part,
> Saying, "Ho, all who weary, enter here!
> There falls each ancient barrier that the art
> Of race or creed or rank devised, to rear
> Grim bulwarked hatred between heart and heart!"[19]

The theme is the expulsion of Jews from Spain by the Spanish Inquisition in 1492. The structure is identical and the dream of utopia remains the same. In the second example, the New World ("the virgin world"), where "doors of sunset part," announced: "Ho, all the weary, enter here!" In these new lands "there falls each ancient barrier that the art/ Of race or creed or rank devised, to rear/ Grim bulwarked hatred between heart and heart!"

The link between the two sonnets highlights the way Lazarus linked her personal odyssey—the Jewishness of her people—to her national self—the mission of America as a model to other nations. Through literature, she connected these two spheres. If it

---

[19] Emma Lazarus, *Selected Poems*, edited by Esther Schor (New York: Library of America, 2005). The best disquisition I know on Lazarus is also by Schor, *Emma Lazarus* (New York: Schocken Books, 2017).

might be said for America to have an owner, it isn't only one who is already here. It might also be the outsider coming in.

What Americans like about immigrants, what Lazarus celebrates in them, is sacrifice. In order to succeed, you needed to give up your past. And in the process of assimilation, you need to leave behind what makes you different: you need to conform, to become docile.

People don't like immigrants who are un-American. A good immigrant doesn't dwell on loyalties: the United States is seen as the one and only love.

So it isn't surprising the degree to which American literature is simultaneously about, and the product of, outsiders succeeding on the inside. Everywhere one turns, authors are outsiders writing about outsiders who end up becoming protagonists.

That might mean foreign nationals. Or it might refer to dislocated voices; for literature, at its core, is the production of unhappy folk: people in discomfort, who don't quite fit in. The act of writing is a form of expatriation as well as expiation.

Consider Isaac Bashevis Singer, a Yiddish speaker born in a shtetl in Poland, arrived to America in 1935, when he was 31. He was shocked at first by the culture, de facto suffering from writer's block for several years. In time he would become one of the most celebrated non-English writer in America, even while attacked by other Yiddish writers for his lewd imagery. His work appeared in *Playboy*, *Esquire*, *GQ*, and, particularly, in *The New Yorker*. Eventually, the Library of America, an esteemed publishing arbitrator of what is and isn't American, would canonize him with a three-volume set of his *Collected Stories* (2004).

Singer's most famous story—he authored more than a dozen novels but his three-hundred-plus stories are in my view his strongest claim to immortality—is "Gimpel the Fool" (1953), known in the Yiddish original as *"Gimpel Tam,"* meaning Gimpel the Simple. It was translated into English by no other than Saul Bellow, himself an outsider born in Canada, and published in the intellectual magazine *Partisan Review*.

In it Singer's protagonist, a naïf who makes his living as a baker in the shtetl of Frampol, describes, in his own voice—the story is in the first person—how everyone around him makes fun of his gullibility.

> I am Gimpel the Fool. I don't think myself a fool. On the contrary. But that's what folks call me. They gave me the name while I was still in school. I had seven names in all: imbecile, donkey, flax-head, dope, glump, ninny, and fool. The last name stuck. What did my foolishness consist of? I was easy to take in. They said, "Gimpel, you know the rabbi's wife has been brought to childhood?" So I skipped school. Well, it turned out to be a lie. How was I supposed to know? She hadn't had a big belly. But I never looked at her belly. Was that really so foolish? The gang laughed and hee-hawed, stomped and danced and chanted a good-night prayer. And instead of the raisins they give when a woman's lying in, they stuffed my hand full of goat turds. I was no weakling. If I slapped someone he'd see all the way to Cracow. But I'm really not a slugger by nature. I think of myself: Let it pass. So they take advantage of me.[20]

Gimpel does let it pass. The story is about how he doesn't pose any resistance. People make fun of him? So be it. He moved on in order not to get angry. Until one day, after an endless list of abuses, he returns home from work to find his wife Elke in bed with his employee. When questioning them, Elke attempts to convince Gimpel that it is all a figment of his imagination.

[20] Isaac Bashevis Singer, "Gimpel the Fool," *Gimpel the Fool and Other Stories* (New York: Noonday, 1957).

This time, however, he has had enough. Soon after, the Devil himself shows up at his bakery early in the morning. He tells Gimpel that not only has Elke betrayed him; everyone in town consistently ridicules him. "It is time to retaliate?" the devil says. What if Gimpel peed in the recently baked bread? Everyone will eat it without knowing....

Gimpel does pee on the loafs. But a few minutes later, he regrets his action. He will not descend to his enemies' level. He chooses then to destroy that morning's bread.

The end of Singer's plot is emblematic. Gimpel leaves Frampol, becoming a wise man who travels the earth. In his journeys, he realizes that everything in this world is an illusion.

That's it!

The date of the story's publication is crucial: less than a decade after the end of the Second World War, and even less time after the creation of a Jewish state in the Middle East. Singer's "Gimpel the Fool" is a tale of displacement, the protagonist, homeless at the end—that is, without an address—travelling from one landscape to another. It is about rectitude and forgiveness in a time of trouble and about the "aterritoriality" of diaspora Jewish life.[21]

Not surprisingly, it became a watershed text in America. Are you maligned? Look the other way. There are better responses than revenge. For a foreigner making his home in New York, whose own relatives perished during the Holocaust, it was a lesson in forbearance.

---

[21] If read from an Israeli perspective, Singer's story is about the vulnerability of the diaspora. In my book *Jewish Literature: A VSI* (New York and London: Oxford University Press, 2021), I reflect on the topic of "aterritoriality" in the works from "*converso*" writers after the Spanish expulsion of 1492 to novels and essays by Sholem Aleichem, Sigmund Freud, Hannah Arendt, Saul Bellow, Isaac Bashevis Singer, and even Israeli authors like Amos Oz and David Grossman.

Or take Vladimir Nabokov, born in Czarist Russia before the Bolshevik Revolution. He lived in England, Germany, and France before moving to the United States. By then he was in his early forties. Yet Nabokov is also at the heart of American literature. Does the embrace of one nationality represents the rejection of another?

Not quite, but it does imply a renunciation, as in the case of Nabokov's ghostlike character, Cincinnatus C., the protagonist of *Invitation to a Beheading* (1935–6). He is about to be executed. Cincinnatus is a metaphor for American complacency. His crime: in his own words, "gnostical turpitude," which implies that others are uncomfortable with him because he isn't Gatsby-like translucent like them. Cincinnatus tries to hide his handicap by feigning charisma but to no avail. He is awkward, unsocial, and, worse, unproud.[22] In a Kafkesque turn, he is scheduled to be decapitated. For there is no greater offense in American than being unwanted.

That is what America announces for those who are maladjusted: nonexistence. The punishment is a delicious metaphor: either you are with us or you are altogether absent. By writing the novel, Nabokov makes a critique of American mainstreaming: the land where the self is king wants you to be reverential, smug, content—in a word, selfless. As an outsider, you must conform. Yet *Invitation to a Beheading* is truly about nonconformity: be yourself, be different, be an outsider, find your voice.

Even though they are seen with suspicion, the land waits for outsiders. They represent hope. It makes room for them even before they might be aware of their place in it. It is the idea of Manifest Destiny: it selects its dwellers before they are even born, making them part of its club even if they are unaware the club exists.

---

[22] Vladimir Nabokov, *Invitation to a Beheading* (New York: Vintage, 1989).

Inside Lazarus's invitation, "Give me your tired," is the potential for exceptionalism.[23] If given a chance, everyone in America is brilliant because everyone is extraordinary. This is the premise of *A Beautiful Day in the Neighborhood*, the popular TV show in which Fred Rogers, who once famously dreamed of becoming a priest before becoming the guru of American parents between 1968 and 2001, welcomed legions of small viewers with the same greeting every day: you're special, you're unique—you're *you*.

In Louisa May Alcott's *Little Women* (1868), one of the dialogues showcases this need to be either everything or nothing:

> "Rome took all the vanity out of me, for after seeing the wonders there, I felt too insignificant to live, and gave up all my foolish hopes in despair."
>
> "Why should you, with so much energy and talent?"
>
> "That's just why, because talent isn't genius, and no amount of energy can make it so. I want to be great, or nothing. I won't be a common-place dauber, so I don't intend to try anymore."[24]

American exceptionalism is scriptural. By being a land where every tongue is spoken, it is a microcosm that functions as a model in the macrocosm that is the world stage. And it takes seriously—to a fault!—its mission to lead others along the way. Plus, exceptionalism is seen as connecting tissue that enhances

---

[23] Needless to say, not only America claims to be exceptional. So does an almost endless list of peoples: in alphabetical order, Australians, Chinese, Egyptians, French, Germans, the ancient Greek, Hebrews (i.e., Israelites), Iranians, Israelis, Japanese, Ottomans, South Africans, Spaniards, and the ancient Romans. In nineteenth-century European philosophy, the term "exception" was synonymous with unique. German thinker Johann Gottfried Herder connected it to the concept of "*Volk*." Two centuries later, that connection remains ingrained in debates about nationhood.

[24] Luisa May Alcott, *The Annotated Little Women*, edited by John Matteson (New York: W. W. Norton, 2015).

social mobility. The ideal version of America is connected with the belief in meritocracy. Talent will bring you up. It will save you from yourself.

That is the premise of F. Scott Fitzgerald's *The Great Gatsby* (1925), the novel whose theme is excellence *par excellence*. Wealth doesn't erase the self; instead, it amplifies it, exacerbating its qualities. Like Howard Hughes and Jeffrey Epstein and like the totemic Charles Foster Kane at the heart of Orson Welles's film *Citizen Kane* (1941), Jay Gatsby, the novel's eponymous gravitation force, with all his wealth sits in a world of riches in Long Island in which his mysteriousness is projected. It is the roaring twenties, a time of overwhelming wealth in America and of sweeping new technology, art, and mass culture; Gatsby throws parties he doesn't attend, until he is infatuated with Daisy Buchanan, whom he knew years previously from volunteer work she and her friends performed with young officers headed for Europe.

Gatsby's charisma is simply irresistible. Even when he doesn't know him yet, the narrator, Nick Carraway, describes him in a wizardly fashion that has come to be recognized as American charm:

> He smiled understandingly—much more than understandingly. It was one of those rare smiles with a quality of eternal reassurance in it, that you may come across four or five times in life. It faced—or seemed to face—the whole eternal world for an instant, and then concentrated on you with an irresistible prejudice in your favor. It understood you just as far as you wanted to be understood, believed in you as you would like to believe in yourself, and assured you that it had precisely the impression of you that, at your best, you hoped to convey.[25]

---

[25] F. Scott Fitzgerald, *The Great Gatsby* (New York: Scribner, 2004).

Likewise, the selfishness of Gatsby—who believes "in the green light, the orgastic future that year by year recedes before us," at times eluding us, although it doesn't matter as long as "to-morrow we will run faster, stretch out our arms farther"—is a punch in the face. It cannot be confused with European self-proclamation. He is new in every sense: a brat, a narcissist, an abuser, and an enabler. His individuality knows no limits. He is exceptional. His death, shot by George Wilson, Myrtle Wilson's husband, is cathartic. Excess brings down boundaries.

Exceptionalism in America has much to do with hypnosis: you make others believe you're a champ, never a loser, always more than you are. This attitude is both individual and communal. Through an ingrained work ethic as well as a sense of entitlement, every American wants to be exceptional. And the country as a whole sees itself as lightning rod.

Exceptionalism is easily turned into an illness. It makes people egotistical, pushing individualism to the edge. And it turns humility into a trap. In America, to be simple, common, unremarkable is to be forgettable. And oblivion is only for the weak, since the mighty, by definition, are memorable.

5. The Epicenter of Narcissism

In the Trump years, egocentrism in America, always a prominent current in the nation's history, has been placed front and center. His personality traits are such that he has no patience for others. It is me, me, me.

An atrocious pandemic is underway, with Covid-19 infecting millions, yet Trump hasn't found time in his busy presidential schedule to mourn with the victims, at the White House, in their respective places, or via Zoom. Empathy isn't part of his lexicon. In fact, he sees compassion as a vulnerability.

It is well known that when in 1981, Trump's older brother Frederick Trump, Jr., died of a heart attack as a result of alcoholism, Donald Trump went to the movies. And when his own father, Fred Trump, was eulogized in 1999, the future president devoted his entire speech to himself, the business deals he had just made and his overall future as a real-estate entrepreneur.

Narcissus, in Greek mythology, is a proud hunter from Thespiae who is known for his beauty. He demanded others to fully love him or disappear from his sight. For his sight, he believed, needed to be devoted to himself alone. Indeed, Narcissus spends his time celebrating his own vanity. He does it by looking at his own reflection on water.

The words "narcissist" and "egotist" are roughly synonymous, at least in America. This is where that character modality thrives, which isn't accidental given the individualist drive the nation is built upon.

There is a normal dose of narcissism in every healthy person. It is when that dose is multiplied to the oomph degree that it becomes dangerous. By definition, tyrants are egomaniacs. They are convinced the world cannot exist without them.

In Latin America, a region whose history is overwhelmed with dictators, there is a literary tradition called *"las novelas del dictador,"* narratives—written mostly by male writers like Alejo Carpentier, Miguel Ángel Asturias, Gabriel García Márquez, Mario Vargas Llosa, and Augusto Roa Bastos, the sole woman author being

Luisa Valenzuela—explore the solipsistic universe where these strongmen build their fortresses.

In contrast, the United States doesn't have *una novela del dictador*, though after Trump it might get one. But as the twenty-first century gets under way in ideologically unstable ways, it isn't impossible that it will need one. Indeed, Trump is better suited to be a fictional character than the leader of the world's richest nation.

In *Democracy in America*, Tocqueville talked of the degree to which Americans are self-made. He was fascinated by the system of government that, while in his own words it was a "tyranny of the majority," also allowed for a model approach to life.

Tocqueville thought that self-interest might be easily misunderstood in America. The township, the family, associations, religion, and beliefs served as social cells. There was, in his own view, a strong sense of self. Yet materialism was the driving force, which resulted in a strong emphasis in individualism and, consequently, on egocentrism.

"Americans owe nothing to any man," Tocqueville wrote, "they expect nothing from any man; they acquire the habit of always considering themselves as standing alone, and they are apt to imagine that their whole destiny is in their own hands. Thus democracy throws [a man] back forever upon himself alone, and threatens in the end to confine him entirely within the solitude of his own heart."[26]

This attitude has prevailed since the birth of the republic. The country wanted to be different from England. And its citizens wanted to be different from common Europeans. Difference was

[26] Alexis de Tocqueville, *Democracy in America*, translated by Arthur Goldhammer (New York: Library of America, 2004).

expressed in the courage to disagree, to be valiant, to toot one's own horn. Yet even in the age of globalism where sameness is the sine qua non of encounters, difference is expressed through simple acts of defiance.

The obsession with oneself is the byproduct of the commonly held religion of individualism. To emphasize who one is, one needs to embrace variance. Literature is the funneling of that variance. Why is a Mexican writer eager to produce a book that shares elements with that of an Egyptian, a Japanese, and a Pakistani? In order to show disparity.

American literature celebrates those defiant acts, small and big. The acts might have to do with talent. Or they might simply be about wanting to live one's life freely. In Nathaniel Hawthorne's *The Scarlet Letter* (1850), Hester Prynne carries a public "A" that catalogues her, in the eyes of the Puritan Massachusetts Bay Colony, as an adulteress. The time was 1642 to 1649. Conceptions of sin were rigid in colonial America.

Prynne's defiance is about individual choice. She has had an affair with Roger Chillingworth, out of which she gets pregnant. As a result, she becomes a target of scorn. The pressure of society over the individual is enormous. Yet heroism is seen as the capacity to withstand it without losing track of one's convictions.

It is unimaginable that Hawthorne would have taken the colonists' side against Prynne, endorsing the contempt against her. Even if the Puritans were all Americans, that position would have been antithetical to what America is: a land of self-determination. The novel immolates the feminine hero, turning her into a revolutionary. At heart she is Quixotic even if her Quixotism is only bringing her misery.

While strictly speaking individualism and egotism aren't synonymous, they share a similar metabolism. The two are about self-absorption. They not only assert a person's capacity to assert unique traits; they also capitalize the pronoun ME before any other.

In *The Devil's Dictionary*, Ambrose Bierce, a journalist, poet, and short-story writer who was a veteran of the American Civil War, describes an egotist as "a person more interested in himself than in me."[27] The egotist is a self-seeker. The entire universe is built around that self. The individualist, on the other hand, cherishes independence without turning the self into a center of gravity. Another drive is to make self-reliance an attitude.

At the core of the egotist's quest is the conviction that freedom was made for no one else. That person is free to the degree to which no one might interfere. Not surprisingly, in a nation driven by money and instant gratification, American literature is about success. That success is measured in dollars. As a writer, to be applauded is to become rich. No other form of gratification is as valuable. It entails a submission to what the audience wants: if the audience wants laughter, bring the jokes; if it wants thrills, untap the horrors.

The egotist, hence, is always bouncing ideas in order to test the waters.

---

[27] Ambrose Bierce, *The Devil's Dictionary, Tales, and Memoirs: In the Midst of Life (Tales of Soldiers and Civilians), Can Such Things Be?,* and *Selected Stories,* edited by S. T. Joshi (Library of America, 2011). Inventively as well as lexicographically, this dictionary is a marvel. However, in my view Bierce's best piece is "An Occurrence at Owl Creek Bridge" (1890). One of the best short stories in American literature, it is about Peyton Farquhar, a plantation owner who, during the American Civil War, is about to be hung from an Alabama railroad bridge. At the moment of death, he is able to see leave his body and see the world. It reminds me of a similar story by Jorge Luis Borges, "The Secret Miracle." This one is set in Prague in 1939.

I have a friend who is the daughter of Indian immigrants. Although she was born in London, the family immigrated to American when my friend was a little girl. She grew up defined by the nation's tenets: make a place for your own, at all cost.

She did, becoming a successful novelist. Early in the mornings over the summer, she and I would swim together across a pond. Before and after, we would share experiences about being immigrants.

But somewhere along the way—in Dante's words that open his *Inferno*: "Nel mezzo del cammin di nostra vita"—my friend woke up to the extremes of the American character: me, me, me. Already a mother with two children, she and her husband took a year off in Rome. The experience was transformative.

She taught herself Italian and, in a relatively short time, she began writing in it. Once that sense of a new home materialized, not only physically but linguistically, she began to look at the United States with increasingly distancing eyes.

Whereas Italy, in its Mediterranean lifestyle, emphasizes camaraderie, America is selfish, putting the I before the WE. The way people engage with each other is frequently as a contest to see who is the best.

Years after her initial Italian sojourn, her children already in college, my friend decided, to the degree possible, to spend all of her time in Rome. For her it was more than a simple choice, though; it was also a rejection. She didn't want to think of herself as part of a country that celebrates self-absorption.

This tension between egocentrism and community is the grease at the core of the American spirit. After all, the nation is also deeply committed to voluntarism, the act of giving to others whatever is achieved for one's own. Although the social eye matters, it is also seen as a thief, taking from us what we most cherish: intimacy, the sense of being autonomous.

It is one of Emily Dickinson's most repeated works—poem #260 (1890):

> I'm Nobody! Who are you?
> Are you—Nobody—too?
> Then there's a pair of us!
> Don't tell! They'd advertise—you know!
> How dreary—to be—Somebody!
> How public—like a Frog—
> To tell one's name—the livelong June—
> To an admiring Bog![28]

The syntax is, well, Dickinsonian: fractured, interrupted, deliberately child-like. And the message is enchanting: fame!—be wary of it, for it will trap you.

Written by a recluse at the apex of transcendentalism in Amherst, Massachusetts, the heart of New England, it is a meditation of the self. Nobody isn't only capitalized; it is celebrated. It is good to be shy, silent, non-advertised. That shyness doesn't translate into absence.

Dickinson's Nobody is a Somebody deliberately choosing the sidelines. She is astute, centered, and knowledgeable of herself. She is different, too. She simply doesn't want to be in the spotlight.

What makes American literature homogeneous is difference. It strives by finding contrast, variation, dispute. It looks at the symphony of voices that pullulate on the street as cacophonous.

---

[28] Emily Dickinson, *The Poems of Emily Dickinson*, edited by Ralph W. Franklin (Cambridge, Mass.: The Belknap Press of Harvard University Press, 1998).

Literature doesn't want to eliminate that dissonance but to exacerbate, to make its stridency urgent, palpable, unavoidable.

Egotism is the opposite force: it thrives in centralizing what's around it. It looks for a single-sided, homogenized viewpoint, shunning anything that is ready to question it.

CHAPTER II

HUCKS R' US

1. Down the Mississippi

Everyone is on a journey in America since America itself is a journey.

Each journey is at once physical and allegorical: we travel in order to leave home but also in order to find enlightenment. The trek matters far more than the destination: in other words, it isn't where we are going but that we are going.

Often the travelers are malcontents. The archetypal journey down the Mississippi by Huck and Jim is a prime example. As such, it is a metaphor of what American literature is about: their expedition is in search of legitimacy, looking to validate their discomfort as an authentic component of Americanness.

In a notice at the outset of the novel, Twain states: "Persons attempting to find a motive in this narrative will be prosecuted; persons attempting to find a moral in it will be banished; persons attempting to find a plot in it will be shot." But we have done nothing else with *Adventures of Huckleberry Finn* (1884): its plot is about the search for an Arcadia for two outcasts.

Starting with Ernest Hemingway, everyone perceives it as the ultimate root, the starting line of American literature not being the indigenous folktales or slave narratives but this pair of escapees, a rambunctious 12- or 13-year-old running away from an alcoholic father and a severe aunt, and a runaway slave.

In the study *Love and Death in the American Novel* (1960), literary critic Leslie A. Fiedler, who was interested in myths, states that "Twain thought of the trip home as a voyage south; but like the earlier writers, too, he felt that trip a descent into hell."[1] Truth is, the journey for Huck is an infatuation with the idyllic quality of childhood: objects for him aren't their actual size, they are either smaller or bigger than they seem.

Released barely two decades after the Civil War, *Huckleberry Finn* was a sequel to *The Adventures of Tom Sawyer* (1876), which is far less readable, in part because it is told in third person with Tom Sawyer as lead, and was therefore designed as innocent entertainment for young readers. There is nothing innocent in the sequel. But Twain missed the mark, or else he expanded his circle, for it is adults who keep infringing on the protagonists' innocence, Huck and Jim.

Huck is boisterous. He is the product of a broken home. He doesn't fit in. Widow Douglass, who has assumed the responsibility of raising him since his father is the town drunk, can't figure out how to anchor him. Huck is ready to sacrifice everything, in part because he has nothing to lose. In fact, at one point he puts it in what might be the best line in the novel: "All right, then, I'll go to hell."

He is humble and enamored with freedom. He doesn't want to go to school because "what's the use you learning to do right when it's troublesome to do right and ain't no trouble to do wrong, and the wages is just the same?" And he wants Jim free because "right

---

[1] Leslie A. Fiedler, *Love and Death in the American Novel* (Naperville, Ill.: Dalkey Archive Press, 1998).

is right, and wrong is wrong, and a body ain't got no business doing wrong when he ain't ignorant and knows better."[2]

As for Jim, who is Miss Watson's slave (Miss Watson is Widow Douglass's sister), he too is full of fears. To others, he isn't defined by his individual attributes but by the color of his skin. Toni Morrison, in *Playing in the Dark* (1992), sees Jim as a metaphor—the Rubicon through which to appreciate the excesses of racism in America, always "expensively kept, economically unsound, a spurious and useless political asset" that remains constant since the age of Enlightenment.

These two odysseys create discomfort. I love teaching it because I love the inspiring quality of Twain's types. And I love how it mimics *Don Quixote* (1605–15) in peripatetic goings-on. But some can't swallow it.

Paul Moses, a professor of clinical psychology at Stanford who conducted research on the connection of the human voice and neurosis, and was also interested in prosody and timbre, couldn't stand the gist of it. Moses told literary critic Wayne C. Booth that "it's hard for me to say this, but I have to say it anyway: I simply can't teach *Huckleberry Finn* again."

Booth quotes him in *The Company We Keep: An Ethics of Fiction* (1989):

> The way Mark Twain portrays Jim is so offensive to me that I get angry in class, and I can't get all those liberal white kids to understand why I am angry. What's more, I don't think it's right to subject students, black or white, to the many distorted views on race on which that book is based. No, it's not the word "nigger" I'm objecting to, it's the whole range of assumptions about slavery and its consequences, and about how whites should deal with

[2] Mark Twain, *Mississippi Writings* (New York: Library of America, 1982).

liberated slaves, and how liberated slaves should behave or will behave toward white, good ones and bad ones. That book is just bad education, and the fact that it's so cleverly written makes it even more troublesome for me.[3]

Bad education? Just the opposite. By the way, a few years back, NewSouth, a publisher in Montgomery, Alabama, brought out an expurgated edition of *Huckleberry Finn* without the n-word. It caused a commotion. Its purpose, apparently, was to allow the book into high schools in the South, where it had been censored for its offensive language. While its editor, Alan Gribben, wanted to make a case for inclusion, his effort backfired, the result of political correctness run amok. The barrage of criticism—who was he to tinker with such an American classic?—was a sign of what has come to be known as "cancel culture."[4]

A nation that sees itself as a refuge from other shores, asking them for the "wretched refuse," "the homeless, tempest-tost," is full of misfits. And look from Scout Finch in *To Kill a Mockingbird* (1960) to Willy Loman in *Death of a Salesman* (1949), from Sal Paradise and Dean Moriarty in *On the Road* (1957) to the duo of Cuban sibling musicians in *The Mambo Kings Play Songs of Love* (1989).

How does *E pluribus unum* work? In what way does the unit become part of the whole and vice versa? The empathy audiences have toward Huck and Jim moves these rejects from the periphery of culture to center stage. The misfits are often the immigrants. The fight between majority and minority voices is at the heart

---

[3] Wayne C. Booth, *The Company We Keep: An Ethics of Fiction* (Los Angeles: University of California Press, 1989).

[4] To me the controversy smelled of fanaticism. It was reminiscent of the either/or conundrum of ideological movements like China's Cultural Revolution and Fidel Castro's Cuba. Alan Gribben never intended to replace Twain's original; his edition was simply meant to be another offering in the marketplace.

of the matter. Those with a different color skin, with an accent, with a different demeanor—Black, Latino, Jewish, Asian, Irish, and other foreigners—exist in perpetual motion, questioning the solidity of the center.

Even within wealth, the misfits are intrepid. Yes, the outcasts, like Christopher McCandless in Jon Krakauer's *Into the Wild* (1996), are often "incasts" turned bitter. Emily Hahn, in *Romantic Rebels* (1967), argues that "the Bohemian who tires of life, who gives up by retirement into insanity or suicide, is not necessarily one who had failed in what he wants to express."[5]

That's the mechanism at the core of American rebelliousness: the automaton suddenly wakes up to ideas beyond the system. Along these lines, H. L. Mencken, the Baltimore journalist, man of letters, and inveterate curmudgeon, thought that "The most dangerous man to any government is the man who is able to think things out for himself, without regard to the prevailing superstitions and taboos. Almost inevitably he comes to the conclusion that the government he lives under is dishonest, insane, and intolerable...."[6]

It is easy to play with the definition of misfit. Perhaps the easiest, most compact one is "anyone who is running away." The nation has as its mantra the conviction that life is fleeting, that individual character is forged through the sorting of obstacles, that arriving at one's end is best done through the sharpening of that character

---

[5] Emily Hahn, *Romantic Rebels: An Informal History of Bohemianism in America* (Boston: Houghton Mifflin, 1967).

[6] One of the best volumes I know of Mencken's work is *The Days Trilogy* (*Happy Days, Newspaper Days*, and *Heathen Days*, plus *Days Revised: Unpublished Commentary*, edited by Marion Elizabeth Rogers [New York: Library of America, 2014]). It shows him as his most acerbic, which was Mencken's prime characteristic as an essayist—and in life in general.

through a combination of tests with the elements and with a society that is as ignorant as it is unforgiving. Americans live in flight: to test themselves, to prove their true worth. They seek rules but living in constant defiance of them. To be successful in America is to be oneself.

American literature celebrates a particular type of runaway: the one with a heart. Hemingway's own *The Old Man and the Sea* (1952) states that "Most people were heartless about turtles because a turtle's heart will beat for hours after it has been cut up and butchered. But the old man thought, I have such a heart too."[7] But if you don't have a heart, you're ostracized.

Among my favorite outcasts in American literature is Gregorio Cortez, the protagonist of Américo Paredes's ethnographic disquisition *With His Pistol in His Hand: A Border Ballad and Its Hero* (1958). It tells the story not only of a reluctant, mythical Mexican-American rebel on the Texan side of the U.S.-Mexican border whose life is upended when an English-speaking sheriff kills his brother because of a linguistic misunderstanding. Cortez, who only knows Spanish, fires back killing the sheriff. He then must escape a major hunt by the American authorities who see him as a threat to society.

Gregorio Cortez soon became "Gregorio Cortez," a myth, a legend. He was turned into a *corrido*, a folk song that is also border ballad—in fact, there are many variations of it—about his ordeal, one that keeps him alive and is still performed today by different artists.[8] Paredes's book is crucial in that offers a perspective

---

[7] Ernest Hemingway, *The Old Man and the Sea* (New York: Scribner, 2020).

[8] The performance by Trovadores Regionales, for instance, features two voices accompanied by an acoustic guitar plucking a simple harmony. Throughout the majority of the piece, the two vocal parts are separated by a

seldom addressed in American rebel literature: the unemployed. How often do American novels explore the plight of this population? Or people on food stamps? Or who may have caretaking obligations? Mental health issues? Or the ones without a sense of self? Very seldom. That's because the allure of literature is to be found in self-drive. No matter what the obstacles might be, a character without self-drive is seen as forgettable. If the environment

---

third, a musical interval used frequently in the creation of harmony. Thirds can be either major, slightly further apart and evocative of positive emotions, or minor, slightly closer together, and evocative of sadness and mourning. The harmonies in "Gregorio Cortez" feature both major and minor thirds, and frequently change from one variety to the other in quick succession. The effect is that of epic tragedy, a song about injustice and heroics told in glorious tradition, and music rapidly swimming out of happiness and sadness. Major and minor chords work together to inspire and describe glory, without diminishing the tragedy and bitterness experienced by Cortez. The song likely owes some of its power and legacy to this harmonious juxtaposition. The corrido does all this without deviating outside of its key signature, creating a cohesive feeling with no notes that sound as though they are not meant to be there. The guitar part is simple, and exists to compliment the vocals without distracting from them.

Another U.S.-Mexican border *foragido*—Spanish for outlaw—like Gregorio Cortez is his contemporary Joaquín Murrieta (sometimes spelled with only one "r"), whose adventures have generated much literature, including a play by Pablo Neruda, *Splendor and Death of Joaquín Murieta* (1967). Other important Mexican-American outlaws are Juan Napomuceno Cortina and Tiburcio Vázquez. I explore the literature about these outlaws in the *Norton Anthology of Latino Literature* (New York: W.W. Norton, 2011).

"Gregorio Cortez" is written in 3/4 time, meaning that there are three beats in every measure and that the quarter note gets the beat, which is common for corridos and characteristic of waltzes. The tempo is fast, and the key signature features three sharps, making this piece in A major and F sharp minor. As it ends on a major chord with a feeling of hope, it is best described as being in A major. Long, sustained notes followed by dramatic pauses allow the singers to catch their breath, and leave listeners on the edge of their seats, waiting for the next part of the story. A film called *The Ballad of Gregorio Cortez*, made originally by PBS in 1983, with Edward James Olmos as the lead and directed by Robert M. Young from a screenplay by Victor Villaseñor, retells the Cortez story from the interpreter's perspective.

defines that character, there is little chance a novelist will pay attention. But if the character, in spite—or better, in the face—of adversity, has grip, even it is deeply buried, there's a chance for the spotlight.

There is another type of rebel: the drug addict. I don't mean it in the addictive sense. I'm referring to American writers who journey through hallucinogenic substances—LSD, mushrooms, peyote, ayahuasca—into alternative modes of consciousness.

One of the pillars of this approach is Carlos Castaneda, whose study *The Teachings of Don Juan: A Yaqui Way of Knowledge* (1968) was originally the author's doctoral dissertation at UCLA.

Like J. D. Salinger and Thomas Pynchon, he is an enigma who deliberately avoided interviews and other forms of public promotion. Yet we know even less about him than about these other two authors. He was an anthropologist born in Cajamarca, Peru, in 1925 who died in Los Angeles in 1998, at the age of 72. He claimed to have an insider's view of Yaqui culture yet his work has been criticized for being anachronistic, empty of any concrete Yaqui references. (Octavio Paz, winner of the Nobel Prize for Literature from Mexico, wrote a prologue to the Mexican edition of *The Teachings of Don Juan.*)

Castaneda was interested in shamanism. His portrait is of Don Juan Matus, the shaman who purportedly introduced Castaneda to an alternative way of knowledge and took him under his wing. He invited Castaneda to ceremonies in which, first as a trainee and then on his own merit, he transformed himself into his personal animal, a coyote.

The type of deception Castaneda engaged in isn't atypical in American literature. The controversy is essentially about authenticity. Is his claim to have a true voice true? Is it trustworthy, accurate, and reliable?

American writers who can't stand conformism, whose role is to subvert, opt for the role of wanderers. The nation's bookshelf is filled with leaving, either temporarily or forever. Staying put would not only compromise their freedom; it would also domesticate their views.

And so, in a centripetal journey, they move out. The world is their oyster. They become like Odysseus in his eternal return to Ithaca. Paul Bowles, who was an American composer, novelist, and translator who spent his life in migration, spending a generous portion of it in Tangiers, explored transience in *The Sheltering Sky* (1949). The novel is about Port Moresby and his wife Kit, surrogates for Bowles and his wife Jane Bowles. New Yorkers in a state of crisis, they wander through North Africa in the hope of resolving their differences. But travel isn't the panacea. Their internal disorientation manifests itself overtly as they put themselves in actual danger.

They are homeless, which means they are without an anchor. Yet they never quite mix with the natives. Instead, they remain stubbornly American, longing for a return to a nonexistent origin. Once you've left the nest, Thomas Wolfe said, "you can't go home again!" And when you do, your perspective is dramatically different. Not surprisingly, a writer's rite of passage is take off, that departure from the quotidian.

American literature is gravitational. That is, its navel is never at the center; instead, it is always wherever the wanderer wants it to be. The whole country sees itself as made of insurgents, protestors, and mavericks: rebels with a cause. Is this an illusion?

Is the ultimate message of American literature that outcasts are embraced by society? Does this really happen in real life? In the end, misfits become mainstream in America. What is on the other side—the neighbor's greener valley—is alluring. There is a forbidden fruit awaiting. It comes in varieties: sex, power, immortality.

American literature is often by outsiders—ambassadors like Washington Irving, reporters like Lafcadio Hearn, expats like T. S. Eliot and Gertrude Stein, renegades like James Baldwin—yet those outsiders end up representing the mainstream. Thus, there is a never-ending dialectic between those that challenge the limits of conformity and the way their challenge is ultimately subsumed to that conformity.

It isn't difficult to prove this point. The fact that that these novels of defiance are staples of the national curriculum in America shows the degree to which they have been coopted by the mainstream. Novels, of course, aren't only escapes. They teach readers how to live.

2. Kids' Lit

On the subject of literature as a manual for life, in this section I want to talk about American children's literature.[9] This is a gigantic

---

[9] I write this not long after the "zero tolerance" policy of the Trump Administration, officially established on the U.S.-Mexico border between April and June 2018 and designed to deter illegal immigration, resulted in the separation of more than 1,100 families. Furthermore, the children of those families were put in cages. Did we forget what affliction is? Are we altogether immune to the atrocities being committed on a regular basis on the border by patrol officers whose last names are just like ours? Do we believe that because this tragedy happens thousands of miles away we aren't complicit? Is this not a moment of reckoning?

More than anything else, who speaks for the children? Do we treat them like cattle because they have no voice? Who gave us permission to separate them from their guardians, to quarantine them in overcrowded camps, to put them in cages?

Have we not learned the lessons from the past, when the children of slaves were sold like merchandise at auctions in front of their own parents, when indigenous families were moved from one reservation to another to make room for land purchases, when Japanese-Americans were interned in camps during the Second World War because of their origin? How about the Holocaust? Wasn't it ignominious enough? Don't we teach these episodes in our classrooms? Have we been doing it mechanically, without insight, simply to satisfy a curricular hole?

Will we have the courage to recognize that "millions of asylum seekers" is an abstraction behind which are real people, each with their own sense of self?

Didn't Robert Frost suggest that "this land was ours before we were the land's"? What did he mean by "ours"? And which land? Is hell part of that land? In what circle of hell is President Trump destined to live in eternity? Will it be one reserved for bullies? For egoists and self-aggrandizing maniacs? Will his own descendants respond to the suffering he inflicted?

How will we answer when as grown-ups these children, trapped in solitude, come back with questions, an endless chain of them, rightfully demanding an explanation? What will we tell them? That we were not paying attention? That we were sold a bill of goods that sounded like a suitable solution, "a final solution"—a wall, a sophisticated army made of machine guns, howling dogs—to an immigration problem run amok? That we had voted a racist into office and couldn't do anything about it because .... Because? Will we again be required to talk of reparations, as if that were the right response to an epidemic of trauma that could have been easily avoided? Will we sound like cowards? And will we tell them we didn't quite understand how dark a period we were living in?

Will they believe us? Will we be brave in our responses? Or embarrassed by the array of excuses coming out of our mouth? Will we blame amnesia—sorry but we don't quite remember? Will we accuse the media for not being more pointed, resorting to explanations like "fake news," forgetting that in the end every nation has the media it deserves?

Have we lost our moral compass? And have we forgotten what Martin Luther King, Jr., said, that injustice anywhere is a threat to justice everywhere? Is justice not what the United States strives for, justice *for all*? Are those wanting to join us beyond its purview? Isn't justice worth dying for?

Isn't poetry what's left when extremist ideologies make people hide behind slogans? Didn't Pablo Neruda say, in "I Explain a Few Things," his illustrious poem about the Spanish Civil War, which he witnessed in Madrid next to friends like Federico García Lorca and Antonio Machado, that the blood of children isn't

industry. About thirty thousand new titles are published every year. Out of about 300,000, this is a whopper that represents a tenth of the overall number of new books. Not only that. The children's book industry is the most lucrative. And the fastest in terms of growth.

Its development in the United States has much to do with the focus on childhood as a formative period in a person's life, which is a twentieth-century phenomenon, thanks in large part to Sigmund Freud and psychoanalysis. In prior centuries, even in the first half of the nineteenth, children's books were almost nonexistent.

America is enthusiastic about children's books. Although there are classics everywhere in the globe (*Alice in Wonderland* in Britain,

a metaphor and that to witness it spilled onto the street means witnessing the death of the future?

Is the plight of one immigrant less worthy than the plight of another? Do we see immigrants as capital only if they arrive with a fat wallet, a doctorate degree, and a Rolodex? What happened to the myth of starting at the bottom? Don't these children whose life is beginning now and their parents who wonder why they brought them into this cruel world want to cross the border not because they want to become an annoyance to us but because the countries they come from were ravaged by tyrannical regimes sponsored by our own government? Or have we become masters at washing our hands from past sins? How many times must these people in need state that were peace and prosperity available where they come from there would be no reason to move? In such circumstances, wouldn't we seek asylum as well?

Who gave Donald Trump permission to say that "our country is already full"? Full of what? Aren't his skittish pronouncements a betrayal of the core values this nation was built on, eloquently in display in Emma Lazarus's sonnet "The New Colossus," inscribed in the plaque on the pedestal of the Statue of Liberty: "Give me your tired, your poor, your huddled masses yearning to breathe free"? Isn't freedom as important as justice? Don't they go hand in hand? And is one person's freedom worth less than another's?

Are we sheer bystanders?

Le petit prince in France, and so on), there is a plethora in the United States: Eric Carle, *Curious George,* the *Berenstain Bears,* and so on.

I will focus on two authors, one from the perspective of translation, the other as an "ethnic" writer whose oeuvre, when canonized by the mainstream, isn't seen as ethnic.

Dr. Seuss, aka Theodor Seuss Geisel, was a genius I had never heard of until I immigrated to America. My experience isn't uncommon. He has sold almost a billion copies in his children's books but reading him in a language other than English isn't joyful. His use of anapestic tetrameter, a form practiced by poets from Lord Byron to Edgar Allan Poe, is unrivaled. But try translating it into other languages. The result is often hilarious in inadvertent ways.

Not long ago, I was asked by the Springfield Museum, in Springfield, Massachusetts, to do a reading of *The Cat in the Hat* in Spanish and English. The experience was exhilarating. There are two versions in Spanish. One doesn't attempt to recreate any poetic pattern; the other does. It is called *El gato ensombrerado.* There is no such word as *sombrerado* in Spanish; roughly, it means "enhatted," which I guess might be defined as "overwhelmed by a hat." I credit the translators, Georgina Lázaro and Teresa Mlawer, for taking liberties. After all, we writers are also inventing words. Shakespeare created "dwindle," "tranquil," "gossip," and "zany." Dr. Seuss, no lesser talent, came up with Grinch to Truffula. Apparently, we even owe him the word "nerd," whose first documented use is in *If I Ran the Zoo.*

For those of us fluent in Spanish, it takes no time to identify where a person is from. I could sense that at least one translator of *El gato ensombrerado* was from Puerto Rico. Finding a "universal" sound in Spanish, one without a local address, is harder than it seems, especially when it comes to orality. I tried doing that in the recording. I adore Dr. Seuss but reading him out loud is not unlike kissing under the effect of Novocaine. Honestly, doing it now, at 58, felt like a crowning achievement of sorts. My hosts couldn't have known that I began practicing years ago, in the nineties, when I became a father. To put it gently, my English at the time was raw and inelegant. I would put my boys to sleep reading Dr. Seuss's stanzas. The experience started as an act of courage and would end up as a form of shame. "Pa, his name is Yertle, not Yurtel," one of them would say. Or in *The Lorax*: "Are you again saying 'tnit' or 'thneed'"?

Just as there is something profoundly English (not *British*) in Shakespeare, Dr. Seuss's oeuvre is an astonishing expression of the elasticity of America, its identity as well as its collective self. Undoubtedly, his stories aren't moralistic yet have an ideology. He's an environmentalist, an anti-consumerist (which is ironic, given the profusion of merchandise his legacy has spawned), and a supporter of democracy and exceptionalism. He had blind spots too, like when he supported the encampment of Japanese Americans during the Second World War.

These contradictions don't deter me. After all, Shakespeare created Hamlet *and* Shylock. And the fact that Dr. Seuss was from Springfield is a thrill. I love the Pioneer Valley in large part because of its residents, permanent and itinerant.

What is *The Cat in the Hat* really about? Published in 1957, it might, at first sight, be about conformity. Two siblings, the narrator and his sister Sally, are alone in the house while their mother is out. It is a rainy day and they are bored when an unexpected visitor, the Cat in the Hat, appears out of the blue. He is intent on entertaining them, displaying all sorts of tricks, including holding their fish up in the air inside its bowl. Naturally, everything he juggles around falls to the ground, creating a colossal mess. What would the children's mother think if she suddenly came back? She does indeed, although by then the Cat in the Hat has made sure things are back in their place.

A classic is a book that changes over time. This one by Dr. Seuss is also about disruption. Perhaps it prophetically announces what the American sixties would be about: upheaval, readiness to upset the status quo. Or *The Cat in the Hat*, as a student of mine once suggested, might be about interventionism. After all, the Cat in the Hat arrives uninvited and creates havoc only to leave the place after creating a superficial reordering. Or might it be a diatribe against immigration, looking at outsiders as interlopers? Not that these approaches were intended by Dr. Seuss. He was a professed liberal democrat who supported Franklin D. Roosevelt. Yet those with different politics have used him to advance their own agenda, as when the line "a person's a person, no matter how small" from *Horton Hears a Who* was appropriated by the anti-abortion movement.

The end of *The Cat in the Hat* is perplexing. From a first-person description, the narrative abruptly becomes an interrogation: And you, reader, what would you do if, while your mother was out, you and your sister witnessed the house being turned upside down? Would you tell her? Would you let her know?

I was too busy controlling my voice when reading it to my boys to deliver the lines with a subversive message, which is what I believe Dr. Seuss wanted. This time around, inside the recording booth, I was in command, infusing the last stanza with a clear purpose: Chaos is just another form of organization! For better or worse, what defines our culture is the dialectic between creativity and destruction. We create in order to destroy and vice versa.

That's what *The Cat in the Hat* means: a saboteur children adore. Dr. Seuss's characters love messing things around, turning them upside down and inside out. This fits the entrepreneurial American spirit: to destroy in order to rebuild and vice versa. They are inveterate disruptors, always looking for reform. One might ask: is Dr. Seuss's message in the book too dangerous? The answer is that sanitized kids' lit is unstimulating. It is unpredictable kids' lit that carries the day.

The maxim applies to Maurice Sendak's children's book *Where the Wild Things Are* (1963), which is an astonishing exploration of otherness that resonates far beyond its intended audience. Sendak, who published it at the age of 35 (although he started it several years before), once said, "You cannot write for children. They're much too complicated. You can only write books that are of interest to them."

The theme of *Where the Wild Things Are* is difficult to summarize. Is it the search for individual freedom? The fright that comes with internalizing one's ghosts? The longing for comfort and a good hot meal after a temper tantrum? Conversely, the arithmetic of the volume is easy to grasp: thirty-seven unnumbered pages, eighteen color illustrations (excluding the cover and title page), 338 words, and ten full sentences—not much for a picture book whose influence has proved immeasurable.

Narrated in the past tense, the plot is about an imaginative little boy named Max who one night makes mischief dressed up as a wolf. In the first section Max hangs a rope, constructs a tent, climbs on books, and scares his dog. Exasperated, Max's mother calls him "WILD THING!" (The dialogue between Max and his mother, sparse and pointed, is always in capital letters.) He retorts,

"I'LL EAT YOU UP," and she sends him to his room without dinner. The setting for the adventures that follow is Max's empty stomach.

From here on the action takes place in Max's room, which transmogrifies before his eyes. Upset by his punishment, Max perceives a forest (looking very much like a theatrical set) growing around him, and he giggles at the sight until "the walls became the world all around." An ocean appears and Max, on his private boat, sails through time and space for several weeks, almost a year, until he reaches the place where the wild things are.

This place may well be Sendak's most stunning creation: a dreamlike but threatening land where creatures "roared their terrible roars and gnashed their terrible teeth and rolled their terrible eyes and showed their terrible claws." But Max doesn't fall prey to these creatures. Instead, he commands: "BE STILL!" and by staring at their yellow eyes without blinking tames them. Max has magical powers.

Sendak presents monsters and wild things as synonymous. The distinctive creatures look somewhat endearing, their features juxtaposing elements from diverse species. Several display recognizable human hands and feet. One has a bull head, another a bizarre rooster's head. A third displays a chest that appears to be indelibly wearing pajamas. The unifying characteristic of all the monsters is their upright position and their big yellow eyes. Soon the wild things make Max their king and he presides over them with a golden crown and a scepter. But although he becomes their ruler, he isn't a tyrant. He plays with them: they all bow to the moon, swing on tree branches, and carry Max on their backs. The monsters honor him by calling him "the most wild thing of all."

In a move that echoes the early section of the book, Max eventually gets tired of the rumpus and sends the monsters off to bed without supper. Then the little boy becomes lonely. He smells good things to eat and feels hungry. He wants to be where "someone loves him best of all"; as a result, he gives up being king.

The monsters don't want him to go, so they threaten to eat him up, just as Max threatened his mother earlier in the plot. Confusing destruction with devotion, they warn that they'll eat him because "We love you so much!" Max refuses to stay and the monsters again exhibit their terrible roars, teeth, and claws. But the boy perseveres. He sails back through time and space until he finds himself in his own room, looking just as it always did. And his supper is waiting for him, still hot. The ending of the book asserts a mother's triumphant love.

Sendak was born in Brooklyn to Polish immigrants. His father was a tailor who told his children biblical stories in dramatically embellished form. His mother was psychologically unstable. His parents, the experience of watching Walt Disney's *Fantasia* at an early age, and the presence, visible and invisible, of relatives whose lives had been touched by the Holocaust defined the young Sendak's world view. The parents spoke Yiddish to him. They often sent him to his room. And his mother called him *vilde khaye*, wild beast.

Some read *Where the Wild Things Are* as a tale about innocence and courage, manliness, or even the rite of passage of a child seeking to define his limits in a world he doesn't yet understand. Others seek a psychoanalytic explanation, looking at the disparity between the authority of the outside world and Max's subconscious desires. A third interpretation, tangentially inspired by Shakespeare's *The Tempest*, approaches the plot through the prism of colonialism and abandonment. Like Prospero the magician,

Max is exiled in a distant land surrounded by the sea. He becomes the ruler of the natives, subduing them, until he decides to leave them behind. Whatever interpretation one chooses (to me, they all seem forced), the book's memorable title invites us to understand Max's otherness at home and abroad.

The volume forms a triptych with Sendak's *In the Night Kitchen* (1970) and *Outside Over There* (1981). *Where the Wild Things Are* has been adapted as opera and recast as a musical as well as a film (with a screenplay by Dave Eggers and Spike Jonze, and directed by Jonze). None of these variations comes remotely close to the power of the original.

Apparently, the first draft of *Where the Wild Things Are* featured horses instead of monsters. Sendak's editor at Harper & Row, Ursula Nordstrom, realizing that the author couldn't draw horses very well (the original title was *Where the Wild Horses Are*), asked him to change the characters into creatures he could ably depict. Sendak opted for lovable monsters that, in his own words, resembled the immigrant aunts, uncles, and cousins who visited his childhood home in Brooklyn and for whom he felt both affection and disdain. He saw them as rowdy and impolite: they "could eat you up." In the opera, these monsters have names: Tzippy, Moishe, Aaron, Emile, and Bernard.

In the realm of children's literature, Sendak's method is revolutionary. He shows only what Max experiences and refrains from moralizing or reflecting on the events. Jewishness is implied: although no reference is explicitly made to it, the entire book is permeated with a Jewish sensibility. Max inhabits his own universe; he resists outside authority; he arrives in alien lands but assimilates the inhabitants' culture so well that he becomes a leader. Most of all, he longs for a return to his origins, the only place he feels truly at home.

Upon publication, *Where the Wild Things Are* received negative reviews and was considered inappropriate for young readers. Librarians often put it out of children's reach. And American parents objected to Max's mother as mean, and disapproved of the way he defied her. But Sendak knew that we are all beasts inside and that such a vision is American at heart.

In children's literature he found a humble, modest genre and made it explode. In a 2004 interview, Sendak said, "People often ask, 'What happens to Max?' It's such a coy question. 'Well, he's in therapy forever,' I reply, 'and has to wear a straitjacket.'"

3. Mending Walls

Given the propensity toward outcasts, the question of boundaries in American literature is never too far. Where do I start and end? What about my neighbors?

"Something there is that doesn't love a wall." This is the first line in Robert Frost's poem "Mending Wall," published in the collection *North of Boston* (1914). The unnamed narrator argues against building walls. Yet his neighbor is insistent, counter-arguing that "Good fences make good neighbours."

Such an approach is prevalent in American literature. In Barbara Kingsolver's *The Poisonwood Bible* (1998), Americans in the Belgian Congo are missionaries that come of age by discovering their Americanness. In Robert Stone's *Dog Soldiers* (1974) they smuggle heroin from Vietnam and in his *A Flag for Sunrise* (1981) they are lost in Central America. Americans abroad are Americans obsessed with themselves, not connected with the alien land but spreading the American gospel, even when doing it upside down.

Through mantras like Manifest Destiny, America has pushed beyond its boundaries: its foremost thought to make the world accept American values, taking over what belongs to others while also patrolling the globe in order to keep neighbors in line.

Superficially, bringing down walls is an American promise. This, after all, is the country of the free. But walls go up at every turn, delineating those that are in and those that are out. To be in is modeled with pride: you are one of the chosen, you are part of the club, you have entered paradise. Those that are out are frowned upon. They are seen as lowly, in the process of becoming.

Arguably, Frost didn't have such allegorical ambitions in the poem. It seems to be based on an experience he had, probably in his Vermont cabin. Yet he is cognizant of the challenges a wall entails as a symbol. It is the same vision presented by George Orwell in "Benefit of Clergy: Some Notes on Salvador Dalí" (1944): "The first thing we demand of a wall is that it shall stand up. If it stands up, it is a good wall, and the question of what purpose it serves is separable from that. And yet even the best wall in the world deserves to be pulled down if it surrounds a concentration camp."[10] Walls themselves are innocent. What do they separate? And in what way do those on each side of them agree to have them in between them?

The emblematic word in Frost's first line is "love." What is it that "doesn't love a wall": nature itself? What is it that "sends the

[10] George Orwell, "Benefit of Clergy: Some Notes on Salvador Dalí," *Essays* (New York: Everyman's Library, 2002).

frozen-ground-swell under it,/ And spills the upper boulders in the sun;/ And makes gaps even two can pass abreast"?

Frost didn't invent American love. He didn't even explore it in full. He was a loner in Vermont in communion with nature. Yet love is the great equalizer in American literature. It is in adult literature as well as kids' lit. Hawthorne, Poe, Edna St. Vincent Millay, and W. H. Auden explored it from myriad perspectives.

In *The Portrait of a Lady* (1881), Henry James, a life-long bachelor— he and his family were at pains not to suggest he was homosexual— who lived a substantial amount of years in England, writes about it eloquently: "It has made me better loving you . . . it has made me wiser, and easier, and brighter. I used to want a great many things before, and to be angry that I did not have them. Theoretically, I was satisfied. I flattered myself that I had limited my wants. But I was subject to irritation; I used to have morbid sterile hateful fits of hunger, of desire. Now I really am satisfied, because I can't think of anything better."[11]

The Beat Generation loved the best. Allen Ginsberg, in *Howl*, says there is "no sleep without dreams of love."[12] The core scene in Frost's poem and its aftermath is about a couple of neighbors. One of them, not Frost's narrator, opts to build a wall that delineates their respective properties. The narrator doesn't quite understand why such wall is needed. The response: "Good fences make good neighbors." Upon thinking about it, Frost's narrator concludes that nature itself doesn't love walls. He then decides to take action.

---

[11] Henry James, *The Portrait of a Lady* (New York: Penguin Classics, 2011). I am in awe by Colm Tóibín's novel *The Master* (2004), in which James's quiet homosexuality is explored.

[12] Allen Ginsberg, "Howl," *Howl and Other Poems* (San Francisco: City Lights, 1956).

He will ask: Why do walls make good neighbors? By the end of the poem, the answer becomes clear, although it is never enunciated explicitly: walls mark the line between what is mine and what is yours. They don't turn those lines into a battlefield; on the contrary, they deter a neighbor from overstepping their boundaries.[13] Therefore, Frost's poem at its core is a manifesto on American individualism.

The opposite of love isn't loss. Nor is it hate. The opposite of love is indifference. And in a country where the limelight is eternal, nothing stings more than indifference.

This brings me back to hate. In American literature, hatred is pervasive. Since the act of developing a narrative is meant to explore moral values, hatred is always wrapped in cautionary paper. It leads to punishment. Yet it is also unavoidable, essential, permanent.

The ultimate anti-heroes in American literature are all haters. Captain Ahab in *Moby-Dick* (1851), Hubert Humbert in Nabokov's *Lolita* (1955), and Nurse Ratched in Ken Kesey's *One Flew Over the Cuckoo's Nest* (1975) are evil in their own way. There are others—the icy Cathy Ames in John Steinbeck's *East of Eden* (1952) and greedy Patrick Bateman in Bret Easton Ellis's *American Psycho* (1991), for instance—but as examples these three suffice.

Melville's villain isn't nature personified in an indomitable white whale, but the captain obsessed with taming it. He is not only excessive and obsessive, a megalomaniac, which is a favorite type in American literature; what he hates the most are his own limitations, the realization that he isn't in control, that he is limited. Captain Ahab's description of the white whale is incisive in its violence:

---

[13] Robert Frost, "Mending Wall," *North of Boston* (New York: Henry Holt, 1914).

"Speak, thou vast and venerable head," muttered Ahab, which, though ungarnished with a beard, yet here and there lookest hoary with mosses; speak, mighty head, and tell us the secret thing that is in thee. Of all divers, thou hast dived the deepest. That head upon which the upper sun now gleams, has moved amid this world's foundations. Where unrecorded names and navies rust, and untold hopes and anchors rot; where in her murderous hold this frigate earth is ballasted with bones of millions of the drowned; there, in that awful water-land, there was thy most familiar home. Thou hast been where bell or diver never went; hast slept by many a sailor's side, where sleepless mothers would give their lives to lay them down. Thou saw'st the locked lovers when leaping from their flaming ship; heart to heart they sank beneath the exulting wave; true to each other, when heaven seemed false to them. Thou saw'st the murdered mate when tossed by pirates from the midnight deck; for hours he fell into the deeper midnight of the insatiate maw; and his murderers still sailed on unharmed—while swift lightnings shivered the neighboring ship that would have borne a righteous husband to outstretched, longing arms. O head! thou hast seen enough to split the planets and make an infidel of Abraham, and not one syllable is thine![14]

In *Lolita*, Professor Humbert, Nabokov's alter ego, is a hater of human mediocrity. He is an aesthete fascinated by the way his mind arranges the world. He doesn't see sin where society places it; he is above moral protocols. He makes his obsession with Lolita—"Lolita, light of my life, fire of my loins. My sin, my soul.

---

[14] Herman Melville, *Moby-Dick; or, The White Whale*, edited by Hershel Parker (3rd ed. New York: Norton Critical Editions, 2018). This, in my opinion, is truly "the great American novel." In its transatlantic reach and encyclopedic ambition, it is also "the great Latin American novel," in line with Julio Cortázar's *Hopscotch* (1963), Guillermo Cabrera Infante's *Three Trapped Tigers* (1965), Gabriel García Márquez's *One Hundred Years of Solitude*, Augusto Roa Bastos's *I, the Supreme* (1974), and Mario Vargas Llosa's *The War of the End of the World* (1981). I find Nathaniel Philbrick's *Why Read Moby-Dick?* (2013) insightful.

Lo-lee-ta: the tip of the tongue taking a trip of three steps down the palate to tap, at three, on the teeth. Lo. Lee. Ta."—look like a redemption not only of himself and the pubescent girl but of the whole humankind.

Likewise in *One Flew Over the Cuckoo's Nest*. Nurse Ratched (her last name a warning if there ever was one) believes in rationality as an endorsement of conformity. In Salem State Hospital, she reigns supreme. Such is her authoritarian zeal that she will put Randle McMurphy and other patients in the asylum through hell. Kesey himself worked at a psychiatric ward. Nurse Ratched is based on a real head nurse. He once recalled running into her years later, at an aquarium, and realizing "she is much smaller than I remembered, and a whole lot more human."

At one point, Nurse Ratched says about McMurphy that no, he isn't extraordinary. "He is simply a man and no more, and is subject to all the fears and all the cowering and the timidity that any other man is subject to. Given a few more days, I have a very strong feeling that he will prove this, to us as well as the rest of the patients." Her authority lies in the way she implements the rules: creativity is disorderly and therefore needs to be disciplined.

This hall of haters is a prime example of American odium. To exist, one needs in America an antagonist of caliber. Borders are useful to separate oneself from that antagonist.

4. Sexual Magnets

In America, the body is an embattled metaphor. It might be a metaphor for the actual human body. It is also one for the whole nation. In that sense, the body is always contested. Who owns it?

How did the body come to be the way it is? What is expected of it? In what way is the body a tool for individual advancement?

The body might be sexually charged. Or gender-specific. Or defined by race. Or be a religious artifact. Or a philosophical standpoint. Or a simple point of reference. In any case, it has substantial implications for geography, kinship, faith, or ideology.

Walt Whitman is the lens through which to analyze the American body. For starters, he was physically massive. He also fashioned himself as an old sage, a kind of biblical prophet. And the fact that he was homosexual adds a layer of meaning to him.

His poetry, like his body, was aspirational. "I sing the body electric," part of the magisterial *Leaves of Grass* (1855), is the prime example. It implies all of these layers. The first section reads:

I sing the body electric,
The armies of those I love engirth me and I engirth them,
They will not let me off till I go with them, respond to them,
And discorrupt them, and charge them full with the charge of the soul.
Was it doubted that those who corrupt their own bodies conceal them-
     selves?
And if those who defile the living are as bad as they who defile the dead?
And if the body does not do fully as much as the soul?
And if the body were not the soul, what is the soul?[15]

The first edition of the book appeared a decade before the American Civil War. Guided by the principle that a book is never unfinished until the author dies, Whitman published subsequent editions of *Leaves of Grass*, amending the text with such vigor that scholars are unsure which of all these versions should be considered

---

[15] This and subsequent quotes come from *Leaves of Grass* are from Walt Whitman, *Poetry and Prose*, edited by Justin Kaplan (New York: Library of America, 1982).

the authoritative, final one in aesthetic terms (sometimes an early edition is deemed more precise, or maybe just more resonant in terms of composition), or else in chronological terms.

Whitman's *Leaves of Grass* fits well into this multifarious definition. How many people have read it from "I celebrate myself" to "I stop somewhere, waiting for you"? A minuscule number. Of course, that cipher is deceitful. A book's value isn't found on the amount of readers it has but on their quality and influence. Whitman's classic is larger than itself: it includes multitudes, from the dead to the unborn. And it contradicts itself, meaning it is fluid, unstable, imperfect.

Audiences read into a classic what they want and *Leaves of Grass* wants to become a body onto itself. It wants readers to react effusively, either in favor or against.

In this volume, I haven't given much attention yet to reviews and other forms of literary criticism. I will do so in Chapter III: "Language and Authority." For now, it is important to stress—though it hardly needs emphasis—that no book appears in a vacuum. No matter how small it might seem to be, and even when there are no reactions, its arrival signals a rearrangement of the nation's shelves.

Early reviews are Exhibit A of the polarized reception. Edward Everett Hale said in the *North American Review*:

> So truly accomplished is [its] promise,—which anywhere else would be a flourish of trumpets,—that this thin quarto deserves its name. That is to say, one reads and enjoys the freshness, simplicity, and reality of what he reads, just as the tired man, lying on the hill-side in summer, enjoys the leaves of grass around him,—enjoys the shadow,—enjoys the flecks of sunshine,—not for what they "suggest to him," but for what they are.

But Charles Eliot Norton, the progressive social reformer, in a review published in *Putnam's Monthly*, said that the poems:

> twelve in number, are neither in rhyme nor blank verse, but in a sort of excited prose broken into lines without any attempt at measure or regularity, and, as many readers will perhaps think, without any idea of sense or reason. The writer's scorn for the wonted usages of good writing extends to the vocabulary he adopts; words usually banished from polite society are here employed without reserve and with perfect indifference to their effect on the reader's mind; and not only is the book one not to be read aloud to a mixed audience, but the introduction of terms, never before heard or seen, and of slang expressions, often renders an otherwise striking passage altogether laughable.

In the Brooklyn *Daily Times*, Whitman, in an anonymous act of self-exploration, critiqued his own oeuvre. "What good is it to argue about egotism?" he said. And added:

> There can be no two thoughts on Walt Whitman's egotism. That is what he steps out of the crowd and turns and faces them for. Mark, critics! for otherwise is not used for you the key that leads to the use of the other keys to this well enveloped yet terribly in earnest man. His whole work, his life, manners, friendships, writing, all have among their leading purposes, an evident purpose, as strong and avowed as any of the rest, to stamp a new type of character, namely his own, and indelibly fix it and publish it, not for a model but an illustration, for the present and future of American letters and American young men, for the south the same as the north, and for the Pacific and Mississippi country, and Wisconsin and Texas and Canada and Havana, just as much as New York and Boston. Whatever is needed toward this achievement he puts his hand to, and lets imputations take their time to die.

Of *Leaves of Grass*, the passage of time has built a steep mountain of other opinions. No consensus emerged but it shouldn't for the animosity around these pages is a statement of purpose: Whitman's poem rejoices in a democratic debate. It wants to be feisty, egregious, grandiloquent. It screams and shouts its preferences and its purported indifferences. As such, it is at the heart of the American experiment: an open book, fluid, intensely contested, a fête of pluralism, a chant for the underdog—gay, black, poor.

Whitman's photographs, particularly in his late age, make him look like a biblical prophet. He is obese and fashions a white beard. He is a sage, a prophet leading the country on the road to enlightenment. His tool is poetry. That is, he doesn't communicate through political speeches or religious sermon, although both are implicit in his message. He uses metonymy and metaphor. He also hides behind them. Let others figure out what I say, he states. Let others interpret my wisdom as well as my ignorance. He remembers Samuel Taylor Coleridge's dictum: "Until you understand a writer's ignorance, presume yourself ignorant of his understanding."

Those who love *Leaves of Grass* love it passionately. They recite portions in citizenship swearing ceremonies, on the Fourth of July, on Thanksgiving Day. It resonates as much as the Pledge of Alliance, the Declaration of Independence, and even the U.S. constitution. One's citizen's hymn becomes the people's secular prayer. There is no God behind it (Whitman was an atheist) and no church to sustain it:

> I hear America singing, the varied carols I hear,
> Those of mechanics, each one singing his as it should be blithe
>   and strong,
> The carpenter singing his as he measures his plank or beam,
> The mason singing his as he makes ready for work, or leaves
>   off work,

The boatman singing what belongs to him in his boat,
   the deckhand singing on the steamboat deck,
The shoemaker singing as he sits on his bench, the hatter singing
   as he stands,
The wood-cutter's song, the ploughboy's on his way in the morning,
   or at noon intermission or at sundown,
The delicious singing of the mother, or of the young wife at work,
   or of the girl sewing or washing,
Each singing what belongs to him or her and to none else,
The day what belongs to the day—at night the party of young
   fellows, robust, friendly,
Singing with open mouths their strong melodious songs.

In fact, it is worth defining a literary classic as a book that is capable of fostering a nation. That is the case of the bible, the Quran, the Ramayana, the Nibelung sagas, and countless others. Whitman's *Leaves of Grass* isn't an anomaly in this list. Its influence has been proverbial, from William Carlos Williams, Simon Ortiz, G. K. Williams, and Philip Levine. But he is also a major force elsewhere, with admirers that range from Pablo Neruda to Salman Rushdie.

One of Whitman's children, in my opinion (though at first sight it might not look like it), is Tony Kushner's two-part play *Angels in America: A Gay Fantasia on National Themes* (1991–2). Expounding a vision of a nation in which its spokespeople are the most vulnerable, the play was a direct response to the AIDS epidemic that spread in the eighties, with particular viciousness in the homosexual community. Part One is called *Millennium Approaches* and Part Two, *Perestroika*.

Kushner uses theater to explore the intersection where the national and personal dimensions interact. The play features recognized historical characters such as Roy Cohn, a lawyer and chief council to Senator Joseph McCarthy during the Army-McCarthy hearings in 1954 as well as a friend of Donald Trump. Cohn, a closeted homosexual, was embarrassed to let the public know that he had contracted AIDS. Another figure is the ghost of Ethel Rosenberg, who along with her husband Joel was convicted of spying for the Soviet Union in 1951.

The themes of immigrant lives, the connection between their children and WASPs (White Anglo-Saxon Protestants), and the agonizing ordeal of illness in gay couples are presented in allegorical ways. Angels visit humans to confront them, to ask for accountability, and to help them deal with the tragedy. In that sense, Kushner plays tribute to Whitman. He uses poetic language on stage to dissect the country's decomposing soul.

At the heart of *Angels in America* is the realization, expressively conveyed, that the national and individual bodies are one and the same. The breakdown and even fetidness of one is paralleled in the other.

While the sexual identity of a writer doesn't define a work of art, that sensibility palpitates in every word. Kushner is a touchtone in gay literature in America, which includes Gore Vidal, Baldwin, Edmund White, Michael Cunningham, and Bret Easton Ellis. Likewise, the lesbian literature produced by Adrienne Rich, Audre Lorde, and Gloria Anzaldúa. Alison Bechtel's graphic novel *Fun Home: A Family Tragicomic* (2006), about her odyssey to find her sexual identity as the daughter of a repressed homosexual and in college pushed the genre beyond its confines into American mainstream culture.

That these explorations constitute an indispensable ingredient in American literature is intimately linked to the LGBTQ push for civil rights that started in the sixties as a liberation movement, took off after the Stonewall riots in 1969, and achieved landmark legislation from the U.S. Supreme Court.

One of my own favorite novels about the American body is Ursula Le Guin's *The Left Hand of Darkness* (1969), a science-fiction meditation on gender fluidity. It is a feminist meditation on transcultural travel. It is about an envoy called Genly Ai from the planet Terra assigned the task of visiting another planet, called Gethen, and persuading it to join a confederation. There are enormous barriers. The population of Gethen has no fixed sexual identity. They are ambisexual. Understanding this fluidity poses enormous challenges to Genly Ai.

The question of the sexualized body is also at the core of another major upheaval in American literature: the censoring of books pertaining what conservatives deem amoral behavior. The sexual revolution, inspired in part by Sigmund Freud's belief that repressed erotic forces generate overall psychological imbalances, took human attraction to a new level. (Think Catullus and Ovid.)

The eighteenth century saw its emergence as a particular branch of literature, which in the following hundred years acquired an established if underground reputation. It was in the twentieth, however, where the underground moved mainstream.

Given how puritanical the nation is, no wonder it quickly gave place to a history of censored titles. It goes without saying that censorship isn't exclusively to America. It is a sine qua non in every civilization. As unpleasant as it might appear, is a mechanism used to set parameters. And it is invaluable in that it inspires a variety of strategies to speak the unspeakable. Jorge Luis Borges, who lived in Argentina under Peronism and was an outspoken critic of Argentine Germanophilia during the Second World War, once defined censorship as the mother of metaphor.

Deemed immoral, dozens of forbidden books in America were European imports, from James Joyce's *Ulysses* to D. H. Lawrence's *Lady Chatterley's Lovers*. Yet America is a machine of eroticism, particularly in literature. Released before the Second World War, Henry Miller's *Tropic of Cancer* (1934) and *Tropic of Capricorn* (1939) are a glimpse of a libertine's life. Indeed, the publication of the former in 1961 by Grove was a watershed moment in the testing of obscenity laws in the United States.

Erotic literature turns bodies into magnets. To be in the erotic realm is to be eager to experiment with pleasure. Once again, Nabokov's *Lolita* is the supreme example. It was written in English; only in 1967 did Nabokov publish it in a translation into his native Russia done by himself. (It is a stilted, uninspired version.) The narrative is purportedly a memoir by an older European man, professor Humbert Humbert, who, a prologue by the fictional John Ray, PhD, an editor of psychology books, tells us, is in prison awaiting trial. The names in the memoir are said to have been changed.) Professor Humbert's crime is his affair with a minor, a 12-year-old "nymphet" called Dolores Haze, who is referred to in the narrative by an assortment of names, including Lo, Lola, and Lolita.

The novel created a scandal. (So did Stanley Kubrick's film adaptation in 1962, with James Mason and Sue Lyon.) The manuscript was rejected by countless publishers until Olympia Press, in Paris, agreed to bring it out. Ironically, the novel is now an American literary classic, among the most important works of the twentieth century.

However, it seems as if the tension between provocateurs and censors has come to a truce. For instance, rather than bringing about scandal, the voyeurism and sexual perversity in the bestselling series *Fifty Shades of Gray* (2011–12), by E. L. James was rather embraced by the status quo. In a sense, that embrace announced a new appreciation of porn: instead of censoring it, let it be promulgated by the marketplace. Its effects are likely to be diluted as a result of overstimulation.

James's work didn't aspire to be sophisticated in its portrait of human emotions. What matters is not what the work says but what the work means. Its popularity showcased the insatiable thirst in America for hedonism.

This change of attitude is the result of the fight advocates for First Amendment rights have put on since the middle of the twentieth century. No need for censorship! Let the reader decide! Within itself, the marketplace has its own censoring mechanisms.

The result is a nation in love with testing the limits of its own body, which often burns like amber.

5. I Am Anger

Looking for beatitude: the pastoral—though surely not with that appellation—is a theme in American literature that implies a religious quest. The word "pastoral" has a double meaning: it refers to the duties of those dispensing spiritual guidance; but is rooted in the keeping of sheep, which is how the ecclesiastic order looks at its congregation. In American literature, the pastoral journey is consequently two-fold: it looks at nature as the theater where the quest for beatitude takes place; and it resists the homogenization of the sheep as a strategy of submission.

Kerouac's *On the Road* (1957) is the ultimate road novel. To be in transition, to be allured, in search of a higher order, makes readers feel a spiritual connection.

A more ambitious quest is Herman Melville's *Moby-Dick* (1851). Upon its publication, the reaction was tepid. It was seen as excessive, another word for unconstrained. Melville's early novels had received a more enthusiastic response, granting him a position of literary importance. But his star was in decline when he published this encyclopedic diatribe about whaling (to me this is perhaps the best Latin American novel ever written outside of Spanish, though it certainly isn't the only one in that terrain).

In fact, one might be able to say that all American novels, at their core, are about a quest.

Edith Wharton says in *Ethan Frome* (1911): "There are lots of ways of being miserable, but there's only one way of being comfortable, and that is to stop running round after happiness. If you make up your mind not to be happy there's no reason why you shouldn't have a fairly good time."

A feature of America is its ever-expanding shelf of protest literature. It showcases an aspect of the nation's character: its feistiness, its insolence, its mischief. In America, this is a quintessential activity, in part because, as Henry Thoreau agues in *Civil Disobedience* (1849), "Disobedience is the true foundation of liberty. The obedient must be slaves."

Thoreau is irritated by the feeling in democracy that a vote is enough to be "active." He criticizes consent and celebrates insurgence. No government, in his eyes, is ever good in nature. It needs to be questioned, confronted. Likewise, he disputes the universal truth that jurisprudence in meant to organize life. "Unjust laws exist," he argues:

> Shall we be content to obey them, or shall we endeavor to amend them, and obey them until we have succeeded, or shall we transgress them at once? Men, generally, under such a government as

this, think that they ought to wait until they have persuaded the
majority to alter them. They think that, if they should resist, the remedy would be worse than the evil. But it is the fault of the government
itself that the remedy is worse than the evil. It makes it worse. Why
is it not more apt to anticipate and provide for reform?[16]

Though with a peculiar bent that made his noncompliance less
about resistance than about being famous as an antagonist, Thoreau
might be considered the father of protest in American literature.
The Founding Fathers were protesters as was Thomas Paine.

There is profit in rebellion. If you wander in search of the
Holy Grail in America, you too will find that "Everything is holy!
everybody's holy! everywhere is holy!" It will not come without
pain. Like Ginsberg, you will witness the apocalypse, witnessing
the frying of the best minds of your generation, all shamelessly
destroyed by madness.

No matter: madness, American madness, is the nation's official
status quo. In order to be an American, you must be nuts. Yes,
everyone is mad. Everyone is in a state of ecstasy. Everyone wants
to enjoy, to have a good time, to be happy. But happiness comes at a
cost. It makes you burst! It dissipates you! It turns you into a robot.

Among the working-class, women, and minorities, protesters
are essential, since it is the only way to carve one's way into the
national space. The parade of dissents—eloquent, inspiring—
is infinite.

For Emma Goldman, for instance, to resist is to march forward.
A Jewish labor organizer whose speeches are a jeremiad against
work-place abuse, she decried marriages as a form of economic

---

[16] Henry Thoreau, "Civil Disobedience," *Collected Essays and Poems*, edited by
Elizabeth Hall Witherell (New York: Library of America, 1997).

slavery. In a speech she delivered in New York City, on July 1897, Goldman posits:

> To all of you I say that it is your lack of courage which makes you cling to and uphold marriage, and while you admit its absurdity in theory, you have not the energy to defy public opinion, and to live your own life practically. You prate of equality of sexes in a future Society, but you think it a necessary evil that woman should suffer at present. You say women are inferior and weaker, and instead of assisting them to grow stronger you help keep them in a degraded position. You demand exclusiveness for us, but you love variety and enjoy it wherever you can get a chance.[17]

And in his *Autobiography* (1965), written by Alex Haley, Malcolm X not only protested the subjugation of Blacks but offered a pathway to change, which was through violence. A more subdued, though equally energetic, alternative was mapped out in the speeches of Rev. Martin Luther King, Jr.:

> I believe that there will be ultimately be a clash between the oppressed and those who do the oppressing. I believe that there will be a clash between those who want freedom, justice and equality for everyone and those who want to continue the system of exploitation. I believe that there will be that kind of clash, but I don't think it will be based on the color of the skin.

The same goes for the political speeches by Cesar Chavez, the Mexican-American labor organizer. He often talked about how the rich in America have money but the poor have time. In his "Plan of Delano" (1965), he announced:

---

[17] Emma Goldman, "Against Marriage," *How Yiddish Changed America and How America Changed Yiddish*, edited by Ilan Stavans and Josh Lambert (New York: Restless Books, 2020).

We are suffering. We have suffered, and we are not afraid to suffer in order to win our cause. We have suffered unnumbered ills and crimes in the name of the Law of the Land. Our men, women, and children have suffered not only the basic brutality of stoop labor, and the most obvious injustices of the system; they have also suffered the desperation of knowing that the system caters to the greed of callous men and not to our needs. Now we will suffer for the purpose of ending the poverty, the misery, and the injustice, with the hope that our children will not be exploited as we have been. They have imposed hunger on us, and now we hunger for justice. We draw our strength from the very despair in which we have been forced to live. *We shall endure.*

There is a hindrance. Protest in America is seen as good, even when the way protesters are manifesting themselves is subpar.

Baldwin, author of *Notes of a Native Son* (1955), puts all this in the context, particularly in regard to American literature, in his essay "Everybody's Protest Novel" (1949), in which he talks about Harriet Beecher Stowe, Richard Wright, and Zora Neale Hurston. He rejects the protest novel as an easy package that inoculates it from all criticism. Regardless of their quality, he says, these novels are allowed to complain because in America they are deemed to bring greater freedom.

This reminds me of an argument made by American critic Irving Howe in his essay "Writing and the Holocaust" (1986), in which he intimates that such is the enormity of the suffering connected with the Holocaust, stating that a text addressing it as bad is morally impossible.

With exquisite style, Baldwin writes:

They are forgiven, on the strength of these good intentions, whatever violence they do to language, whatever excessive demands they make of credibility. It is, indeed, considered the sign of a frivolity so intense as to approach decadence to suggest that these books are both badly written and wildly improbable. One is told to put first things first, the good of society coming before niceties of style or characterization. Even if this were incontestable—for what exactly is the "good" of society?—it argues an insuperable confusion, since literature and sociology are not one and the same; it is impossible to discuss them as if they were. Our passion for categorization, life neatly fitted into pegs, has led to an unforeseen, paradoxical distress; confusion, a breakdown of meaning. Those categories which were meant to define and control the world for us have boomeranged us into chaos; in which limbo we whirl, clutching the straws of our definitions. The "protest" novel, so far from being disturbing, is an accepted and comforting aspect of the American scene, ramifying that framework we believe to be so necessary.[18]

As Baldwin puts it: "'As long as such books are being published,' an American liberal once said to me, 'everything will be alright.'"

Now that's an American stance.

Perhaps the most important one is Herman Melville's story "Bartleby the Scrivener" (1953), about the eponymous ghost-like copier of legal documents. Bartleby, who works at Wall Street, is a resister: "he prefers not to." The line is a battle cry for subversion. To achieve what? It is unclear, since Bartleby doesn't appear to have either motive or ideology. And that, precisely, is what makes him saintly: he refuses to fit in.

Ah, Bartleby! Ah, America!

Deep inside a rebel is the desire to reconfigure the idea of one's own home. And if American literature is about anything, it is about finding that elusive home. It is a bookshelf in which everyone sees themselves reflected, where the "I" become a "we."

---

[18] James Baldwin, "Everyone's Protest Novel," *Collected Essays: Notes of a Native Son, Nobody Knows My Name, The Fire Next Time, No Name in the Street, The Devil Finds Work, and Other Essays*, edited by Toni Morrison (New York: Library of America, 1998).

In itself, the idea of a reconsidered home—and its reverse, homelessness—serves as a leitmotif. It is everywhere, from Thomas Wolfe's *You Can't Go Home Again* (1934) to John Steinbeck's *The Grapes of Wrath* (1939) to Carson McCullers's *The Heart Is a Lonely Hunter* (1940) and Dorothy Allison's *Bastard Out of Carolina* (1992). In each, an individual or a group, exiled from a painfully specific place for an assortment of reasons—aesthetics, character, faith, and labor, among them—explore their condition as pariahs.

One of my favorite coming-of-age novels is Julia Alvarez's *How the Garcia Girls Lost Their Accents* (1991). It explores this condition—rebellion and homelessness—with elasticity. Through shifting narratives, the Garcia sisters, new arrivals from the Dominican Republic, struggle with their parents—an imposing father, a dreamy mother—as they build a space of their own in America. They are all unique: one is prone to anxiety, another is insolent to the point of disobedience. Home, where is it? In Santo Domingo, with its deeply held traditions, where women have little room to express themselves? In America, where too much freedom might result in perdition?

In losing their accent, the Garcia sisters acquire another language: they learn to be American. That learning gives them a sense of value, even though they are constantly in danger of alienation. Their home, they conclude, is a middle-ground, a bit here and a bit there.

Coming to terms with what is home is infused with danger, though. As in the biblical vision of Genesis, there are prohibitions to respect, otherwise you become an outcast. America isn't only where you build a house but where you create a home. That home is never static; it changes as time evolves. The tension between these two poles often comes to a boil.

That give-and-take between reverence and rejection defined the American home: as Annie Dillard puts it in her autobiographical meditation *Pilgrim at Tinker Creek* (1972), it is a place at once profane and sacred.

In the tradition of nature writers that includes Thoreau, along with John Muir, Edward Abbey, Wendell Berry, and Barry Lopez, Dillard turns nature itself into a home. She states:

> I am a frayed and nibbled survivor in a fallen world, and I am getting along. I am aging and eaten and have done my share of eating too. I am not washed and beautiful, in control of a shining world in which everything fits, but instead am wandering awed about on a splintered wreck I've come to care for, whose gnawed trees breathe a delicate air, whose bloodied and scarred creatures are my dearest companions, and whose beauty beats and shines not in its imperfections but overwhelmingly in spite of them.[19]

If reconfiguring that sacred and profane place called home is an uphill battle, losing it is almost unfathomable. Elizabeth Bishop's poem "One Art" (1976), following the structure of a villanelle, was published in *The New Yorker*. It is about the pitfalls of materialism. There are few American poems I feel more connected with.

Bishop starts by asserting that the art of losing is a constant feature in America—and everywhere else as well—but never as a zero-sum game. We look at life as a series of additions, a sum of experience, of insight, of knowledge. Yet things seem poised to disappear. It doesn't matter, since loss isn't a big deal. In fact, she recommends losing things—things, names, a house you love, a continent, a voice, a gesture—as a strategy, since the less we have the freer we become. Indeed, all things in the world want to be lost;

---

[19] Annie Dillard, *Pilgrim at Tinker Creek* (New York: Harper, 2013).

that's their nature. They have no loyalty to anything or anyone. We come close to them, and then, with equal humility, they vanish.

Ownership, Bishop suggests, is about nothing but control. Why should we be so eager for it when the opposite is natural: not to have, not to be entitled to claim items as belonging to us? In the end, she delivers a call to poets as well: write in other voices to separate yourself from the world. Apparently, she reworked "One Art" countless times, producing at least seventeen versions of "One Art." They had titles like "How to Lose Things," "The Gift of Losing Things," and "The Art of Losing Things." As she revised, she concentrated on the rhythm, tweaking every word, and adjusting the content accordingly. She agonized over which version to allow. Is the one we know as the final the best one? And does it matter?

Literature, clearly, is also a form of control—until it isn't. The last line is a command: the art of losing isn't hard to master "though it may look like (*Write* it!) like disaster."[20] Bishop is unequivocal: to succeed, literature must let go.

---

[20] Elizabeth Bishop, "One Art," *The Poems of Elizabeth Bishop* (New York: Farrar, Straus, and Giroux, 2015).

CHAPTER III

LANGUAGE AND AUTHORITY

1. Forever Young

Youth in America is enshrined. I referred to this dimension, in passing, in the discussion of erotic literature. I want to go further now. The young are at the center of everything: they keep the nation on its edge. And they move language forward, revamping it at all times.

Indeed, the young in America speak with absolute freedom. There are no restrictions, no limits. They push for new fashion, they coin new words, and they constantly look for new adventures. George Bernard Shaw once said that "youth is wasted on the young." He surely said it out of jealousy.

In any case, novelty sells in America. "A novelty loses nothing by the fact that it is a novelty," Mencken argued. "It rather gains something, and particularly if it meets the national fancy for the terse, the vivid, and, above all, the bold and imaginative."[1] This is because the plasticity of American literature knows no limit. Writers endow themselves with the right to push it to its limits.

---

[1] This and subsequent quotes are from Mencken, *The American Language: An Inquiry into the Development of English in the United States* (New York: Alfred A. Knopf, 1946).

One finds just about everything in the pages of books: doodles, maps, photographs, etc. Mostly, though, it is extraordinary how language appears capable of capturing the entire world, a world in a permanent state of flux, a world that is nervous, unsettled, in a state of constant reconfiguration.

Advertising and popular culture—singers, movie and TV entertainers, writers—is the engine for change. An anchoring example is the way Michael Jackson helped change the meaning of the word "bad." Prior to him, the traditional, age-long understanding of "bad" was as the opposite of "good." Rooted in Black lingo, Jackson, with his album *Bad* (1987), which includes songs like "The Way You Make Me Feel" and "I Just Can't Stop Loving You," gave it a hundred-and-eighty-degree twist, bringing it to be a positive response.

The language used in Hollywood films comes about from the dialectical relationship between society and the screen: what is said on the streets makes it into Martin Scorsese's *Taxi Driver* (1976), *Raging Bull* (1980), *Goodfellas* (1990), *The Departed* (2006), *The Wolf of Wall Street* (2013), and *The Irishman* (2019). And vice versa, whatever Scorsese inserts in his narratives makes people speak American English differently.

The same thing goes for literature, especially literature targeting young adults. It is enough to take a cursory look at how popular young-adult novels are in America to understand the degree to which a hip, present-driven language changed rapidly even within the span of a single generation.

Take the *Hardy Boys* mystery novels, created by publisher Edward Stratemeyer and written by ghostwriters under the pseudonym of Franklin W. Dixon. They debuted in 1927. The prose was simple. Stratemeyer wasn't a publisher but a packager. His objective was to entertain young boys through whodunits. The success of the series was tremendous. But the writing was nondescript, even mechanical. And the books were also filled with racial stereotypes.

Yet the Hardy Boys shaped young American men in the twentieth century. Not only did their interest in mysteries implanted in their readers the sense that the universe is ruled by mysteries awaiting a rational solution—the source of such an approach is Edgar Allan Poe's "The Murders in the Rue Morgue" (1841)—but the simple, straight, matter-of-fact, unadorned, Hemingwayesque parlance.

Their counterpart, the Nancy Drew novels, first published in the thirties and written by a number of ghostwriters under the pseudonym Carolyn Keene, had a similar impact. It isn't impossible to trace the roots of the Second Wave of feminism—works like Betty Friedan's *The Feminine Mystique* (1963) and Gloria Steinem's journalism and her books such as *Outrageous Acts and Everyday Rebellions* (1983)—to the woman sleuth sorting out the conundrums they face.

The vision that life is a cut-throat, Darwinian competition is found in popular young adult dystopian series like Suzanne Collins's trilogy *The Hunger Games* (2008), *Catching Fire* (2009), and *Mockingjay* (2010). The colorfulness they display, the vision that life is a media-driven contest about the survival of the fittest and the lexicon they feature highlighting that survival, serve as a roadmap for audiences in their existential approach.

Almost from the outset in the nation's history, American literature focused on young readerships. Noah Webster, the lesser known of the nation's Founding Fathers, devoted his early career, immediately after graduating from Yale, to literacy efforts for the young such as the *Blue-Back Spelling Book & New England Primer* (1783).

His professed mission was two-fold: to teach young Americans how to spell; and—this he would realize in subsequent years—to make sure American English was its own concoction, distinguishable from British English.

In time, American literature for young people would become quite ambitious. At its heart are Mark Twain's portraits of Tom Sawyer and Huckleberry Finn. Even though in some way they were *The Hunger Games* of the nineteenth-century, they are, or at least the second novel is, far more complex, particularly when it comes to language, as I mentioned in Chapter II, Section 1: "Down the Mississippi." They surely use a basic, ordinary language but Twain's understanding of what is basic is dramatically different. He toys with American dialect in a playfully subversive way, giving voices not only to Huck, who narrates the story, but, through dialogue, to Jim, whose language is that of slavery.[2] By doing so, it is unquestionable that audiences felt they had been given permission to speak their mind in their own "broken" tongue, using a non-standard lexicon to convey it.

Another watershed novel for young adults in America is J. D. Salinger's *The Catcher in the Rye* (1951), which still sells about a million copies annually. Originally published in serialized form in 1945 and 1946, its first-person narrator, the 16-year-old protagonist Holden Caulfield, is a misfit. He lives in Southern California, near Hollywood. His attitude toward the world is antagonistic. He dislikes just about everyone around him.

---

[2] This parlance is extremely difficult to translate. It brings to mind a line by Don DeLillo in an interview titled "This Is What I See": "When I get a French translation of one of my books that says 'translated from the American', I think, 'Yes, that's exactly right'" (*The Guardian*, August 7, 2010).

That rudeness, the ostracism young people feel, is perfectly captured by Salinger. That, in my view, is why the novel is so popular:

> Among other things, you'll find that you're not the first person who was ever confused and frightened and even sickened by human behavior. You're by no means alone on that score, you'll be excited and stimulated to know. Many, many men have been just as troubled morally and spiritually as you are right now. Happily, some of them kept records of their troubles. You'll learn from them—if you want to. Just as someday, if you have something to offer, someone will learn something from you. It's a beautiful reciprocal arrangement. And it isn't education. It's history. It's poetry.[3]

Indeed, young adult books in America—Sylvia Plath's *The Bell Jar* (1963), Maya Angelou's *I Know Why the Cage Bird Sings* (1969), or Sandra Cisneros's *The House on Mango Street* (1991)—are benchmarks that define one generation after another.

They are invariably designed about a confrontation between the "I" and the "them." The "I" is idealistic and misunderstood yet ready to embrace freedom and seize the day. Or better, to recalibrate freedom in a way that makes the new day feel different.

American literature is, first and foremost, the words it is made of. Those words are in eternal flux. They are nervous; they are disobedient; they never stay still.

2. Of Dictionaries and Academies

Published during the colonial period, the ancestors of what we consider today a dictionaries of American English were unoriginal.

---

[3] J. D. Salinger, *The Catcher in the Rye* (New York: Little, Brown & Co., 1991).

It wasn't until Noah Webster came along with *An American Dictionary of the English Language* (1828) that the nation got the dictionary it deserved. Or at least, an early version of it. (Webster published his first dictionary in 1806.) The title itself is emblematic: the lexicon is American, the tongue British. Inside the volume, there's a push-and-pull between these two turfs. How can English become native to the New World?

Webster was an auspicious figure. In order to trace etymologies, he is said to have learned twenty-six languages, including Hebrew, Greek, and Latin. He was astute in his appreciations of Old (i.e., Anglo-Saxon) and Middle English. But Webster wasn't an original. His dictionary is rather trite. It took inspiration from the far more adventurous *A Dictionary of the English Language* (1755), by Samuel Johnson, which remains not only an astonishing compendium but also a work of individual savvy. Johnson is often described as a doctor although he didn't receive any such degree.

The distinction is fitting. In my mind, no other dictionary in any tongue comes close to his not only in smarts but in wits. A few of his definitions are ageless: lexicographer, for instance, is "a writer of dictionaries; a harmless drudge, that busies himself in tracing the original, and detailing the signification of words."

Johnson is astonishingly punctilious (in today's world he would probably receive a diagnosis of Asperger's syndrome, which says as much about him as it does about the elasticity of this type of diagnosis). Webster is not only flat by comparison; he relies heavily on Johnson in his approach to the language, in the structure of his dictionary, and also in more than a handful of the definitions. He has even been accused of plagiarism. Regardless of the position one takes in that regard, his dependency on the doctor is symbolic: for the United States, independence from England meant a new start. Webster himself was enamored with that idea. His freedom was still in its infancy.[4]

Webster is the father of American lexicography. It was fortuitous that after his death in 1843, George and Charles Merriam, who lived in Springfield, Massachusetts, purchased the rights to his lexicon. The partnership would eventually be behind the famous *Merriam-Webster Dictionary*, which, along with the *Oxford English Dictionary*, is the most important English-language word book.

Yet there is a dramatic difference between the two: whereas the OED is the product of a university press, *Merriam-Webster* is a commercial enterprise. It thus needs to survive through unique strategies having to do with the marketplace.

---

[4] Fascinatingly, in *An American Dictionary of the English Language*, Webster defines the word "God" thus: "God GOD, noun [Saxon god; German gott; Dutch god; Swedish and Danish gud; Gothic goth or guth; Pers. goda or choda; Hindoo, khoda, codam. As this word and good are written exactly alike in Saxon, it has been inferred that God was named from his goodness. But the corresponding words in most of the other languages, are not the same, and I believe no instance can be found of a name given to the Supreme Being from the attribute of goodness. It is probably an idea too remote from the rude conceptions of men in early ages. Except the word Jehovah, I have found the name of the Supreme Being to be usually taken from his supremacy or power, and to be equivalent to lord or ruler, from some root signifying to press or exert force. Now in the present case, we have evidence that this is the sense of this word, for in Persic goda is rendered dominus, possessor, princeps, as is a derivative of the same word. See Cast. Lex. Col. 231.] 1. The Supreme Being; Jehovah; the eternal and infinite spirit, the creator, and the sovereign of the universe. God is a spirit; and they that worship him, must worship him in spirit and in truth. John 4. 2. A false god; a heathen deity; an idol. Fear not the gods of the Amorites. Judges 6. 3. A prince; a ruler; a magistrate or judge; an angel. Thou shalt not revile the gods, nor curse the ruler of thy people. Exodus 22. Psalm 97. [Gods here is a bad translation.] 4. Any person or thing exalted too much in estimation, or deified and honored as the chief good. Whose god is their belly. Philippians 3."

At any rate, there are plenty of important dictionaries in America,[5] to the point that it is fair to say that the nation sees in its language the ups and downs of its reputation.

[5] As I stated in "Notes on Latino Lexicography" (*The Oxford Handbook of Latino Studies*, 2020): "Words are time codes. In their essence, they contain the DNA of the people that created them. Only when seen hastily are they stupid."

I think of myself as a philologist, although I am well aware of how out of fashion the term has become. It used to be that anyone interested in the partnership between language and literature was called a philologist. Now these two fields are divorced. We refer to their respective endeavors with fancier terms, such as linguistics and literary criticism. It is a shame that their compatibility is no longer required. We all suffer as a result. In the Hispanic world, lexicography has little cache.

According to the *Oxford English Dictionary*, this branch of knowledge "deals with the structure, historical development, and relationships of a language." No language exists in a vacuum: it manifests itself in the act of telling something; to isolate language from content is to forget its true worth.

It is less controversial to become a scholar of major languages rather than of those considered minor. A major language (English, Mandarin, Spanish, French, German, etc.) is standardized. Its most ideologically contested quality is that it is imperial, usurping space from other, smaller tongues. Minor languages are the purview of a small numbers of users. They exist like endangered species, in a state of suspended continuity.

I love words just as much as I love narrative. This devotion strive from my Jewishness. I grew up in an environment where literacy was the epicenter. The way to connect to the past was through a commitment to books. I don't remember being an avid reader when I was a child; that appetite came later, when I was in my late teens. Still, my parents surrounded themselves with culture: books, plays, film, music. There wasn't a moment in the day when someone wasn't in the middle of telling a story.

Narrative is the oxygen that makes culture breathe. Narrative isn't only story, though; in other words, it isn't only the "what happens" but the "how it is said to happen," meaning that a narrative is always delivered in language and that form and content are one. A successful story not only depends on the sharpness of its plot. The language that plot takes is equally crucial.

Of course, language itself tells a story, too: the story of its subjects and predicates, its verbs and nouns and adjectives, its punctuation, and, in equal measure, the blank space—silences—between signs within a sentence. Separating story from language is like divorcing oil from water. Yet people seldom look at the two together. They focus almost exclusively on action.

This is because the American language is extraordinarily expansive. Although it inherited this attribute from British English, it has pushed it to the next level. Not that it refuses to acknowledge its debt to England. That commitment is strikingly clear when one considers the role Shakespeare plays in America.

In comparison, there is little interest for Early and Middle English. Authors such as William Caxton, Miles Coverdale, Thomas Mallory, William Tyndale, and John Wycliffe aren't in America's consciousness. *Beowulf* and Geoffrey Chaucer's *The Canterbury Tales* are but, again, they pale in comparison to the Bard.

His marketability is such that American publishers can't get enough of him. His plays are constantly being staged. Students

I am dismayed by the degree to which, after the basics are learned in elementary school, the study of language in all its complexity is abandoned by our education system. I am talking not only of the industrialized nations but of developing countries as well. We would do better on multiple levels if we spent more time looking at words from multiple perspectives. It would make us aware of their limitations as well as their potential. It's a tenet of life that there is much that cannot be said properly; the most challenging intellectual task we have in front of us is *to say things clearly and eloquently*.

Those two characteristics are expressions of refinement. That noun, unfortunately, connotes elitism these days. To express oneself in convoluted fashion doesn't seem to be a sin anymore, although it ought to be. I'm not only referring to speakers with limited education but to everyone. In fact, the situation, in my view, is worse among the educated, including academics. Ever tried analyzing the sense of time in Shakespeare's *Macbeth* (1606)? It might be more obscure than the play itself.

All this is understandable. Ours is an age that looks at language in utilitarian terms. Its function is to convey meaning in quick, packable fashion. Speaking intelligently, matching image and word, takes experience. The accumulation of that experience is what is known as maturity. Maturity in language is linked to maturity of mind and vice versa. By the way, I am aware these comments aren't politically correct. This doesn't make them less true.

I am not a nostalgist who believes the past is better. Quite the contrary, I'm infatuated with the changes the present offers us. Being clear and eloquent is a requirement of any period. It accelerates progress.

read them in high school. It doesn't matter that the language feels old. Actually, that's the point. Americans see Shakespeare as their source.

In any case, American English dances to an evangelical beat, going anywhere and everywhere with a shameless sense of boundlessness. That traction, at once barbaric and civilized, goes hand in hand with the country's imperial dreams: it makes it believe in its own endless possibility.

The rest of the world is turned on by its jazziness. The fact that American literature is conveyed in it makes its content appealing. (I will return to this topic in Chapter IV, Section 4: "Born Translated.")

Does that jazziness sometimes verge on the chaotic? Who legislates its well-being? Why isn't there in English an institution that is the equivalent of France's *Academie française,* Italy's *Academia de la Crusca,* and Spain's *Real Academia de la Lengua?*

The debates among the founders in the Federalist Papers around the crafting of the U.S. constitution frequently neglects a prime fact: they are all written in the Queen's English. Yet the discussion of what will make the language American is at the heart of the experiment that will become America.

John Adams, the nation's second president, believed American English ran the risk of "going to the dogs" unless it was protected from abuse by the masses. He proposed the formation of an institution like the French have had since 1634, endowed with safeguarding it. Yet in a nation infatuated with democracy—"of the people, by the people, for the people"—such a lofty enterprise was sure to run against a wall.

Since, as I said in the opening chapter, in America the past is constantly being reimagined, American English likes to perceive itself as ahistorical. Or better, it likes to imagine the language where it pleases it, no matter how anachronistic those reveries might be. I once stumbled upon a misquotation attributed to a governor of Texas who was asked if the bible ought to be taught in Spanish to non-English speakers. She said that "if English was good enough for Jesus, then it's good enough for me." The fact that the anecdote is apocryphal makes it all the more enticing.

The mother source, England, is the foundation that has sold part of its property for cheap. The mortgage on the sale is small. There are no real obligations. That's why Americans do with English what they please when they please. They are wild, reckless, and irresponsible. British comedian Stephen Fry likes to boast: "Look, we gave you a perfectly good language and you fucked it up."

There have been repeated attempts to create an Academy of English, first in England, then in the United States. Intellectuals in England like Daniel Defoe and Jonathan Swift passionately debated the issue, and politicians on this side of the Atlantic, including Thomas Jefferson and others, in a document called "Constitution of the American Academy of Language and Belle Lettres" (January 11, 1821), suggested its function to be:

> to collect, interchange, and diffuse literary intelligence; to promote the purity and uniformity of the English language; to invite a correspondence with distinguished scholars in other countries speaking this language in connection with ourselves; to cultivate throughout our extensive territory a friendly intercourse among those who feel an interest in the progress of American literature, and, as far as may depend on well-meant endeavors, to aid the general course of learning in the United States.[6]

---

[6] Thomas Jefferson et al., "Constitution of the American Academy of Language and Belle Lettres" (January 11, 1821), *The Papers of Thomas Jefferson: Retirement Series* (2005).

In an age in which immigrants get blamed for not "becoming" Americans fast enough, the need for such institution is often invoked. Linguistic academies are intimately linked to nationalist ideologies. For instance, the Academy of the Hebrew Language came about as the State of Israel consolidated its status as a free country.

At any rate, writers do with the language whatever they want. Dr. Seuss is a perfect example. So are Twain, Henry Roth, and Faulkner. They push it to its limits, breaking it into fragments only to reassemble it again.

The *Adventures of Huckleberry Finn* is written, in part, in a nonexistent dialect.[7] Twain fancied Jim's language out of fantasy. It isn't an ethnographic recreation of the parlance of runaway slaves in the Mississippi delta. He had an ear for dialect but only an ear. In spite of his closeness with Blacks, he didn't come from the inside. He was a brilliant ventriloquist. All ventriloquists are impostors. They pretend to speak for themselves and also for a dummy. The dummy is the one that garnishes all the attention while the ventriloquist is lip-tied.

All national languages are tested by jargon, dialects, sociolects, and creolized variations. Those tests manifest themselves in literature. Some countries dismiss them as dispensable while others endorse them as recalibrations of the standard. America is among the latter. In my opinion, among the most admirable concoctions of American English are parts of Henry Roth's *Call It Sleep* (1934). It is the story of David Schearl, a 6-year-old immigrant boy from Galicia, a territory in Poland that often changed sides in the

---

[7] The Columbia University sociolinguist Max Weinreich, author of *History of the Yiddish Language* (1980), stated—in Yiddish—that *"a shprach eez a deealekt mit an armee un flot,"* a language is a dialect with an army and navy.

twentieth century. David and his mother Genya arrive in New York, where they meet David's aloof father Albert. They settle in the Jewish ghetto of the Lower East Side.

Roth's bildungsroman follows David's awakening. His encounters with a Hebrew teacher, friends, and neighbors are presented to his impressionable eyes. As a newcomer, his language isn't quite English. And, as he assimilates, it isn't his native Yiddish either. *Call It Sleep* features lengthy segments in a hybrid known as Yinglish (it also goes by "Anglish"):

> "It still c'n go," Yussie gravely enlightened him.
>
> David sat down. Fascinated, he stared at the shinning cogs that moved without moving their hearts of light. "So wot makes id?" he asked. In the street David spoke English.
>
> "Kentcha see? Id's coz id's a machine."
>
> "Oh!"
>
> "It wakes op mine fodder in de mawning."

Elsewhere, there are entire transliterations of Hebrew:

> "Begin," he said. "Ma tovu."
>
> "Ma tovu oholeha Yaakov meshkanoseha Yisroel." He poured the sounds out in a breathless, chaotic stream. "Va ani berov hasdeha awvo basecha eshtahave el hahol kodshehe beyeerosehaw."[8]

In other parts of *Call It Sleep*, there are contractions, vowel omissions, double negatives, an abundance of "so", frequent "nu?", and added "-ed" endings to irregular verbs in the past tense.

Another example is Zora Neale Hurston's *Their Eyes Were Watching God* (1937). At one point, a nanny says to the protagonist, Janie: "You

---

[8] Henry Roth, *Call It Sleep* (New York: Delacorte, 1963).

answer me when ah speak. Don't you dare sat dere poutin' wid me after all I done went through for you."[9]

Or take this translation into Spanglish, the mix of Spanish and English, of Part I, Chapter 1 of *Don Quixote*:

> In un placete de La Mancha of which nombre no quiero remembrearme, vivía, not so long ago, uno de esos gentlemen who always tienen una lanza in the rack, una buckler antigua, a skinny caballo y un grayhound para el chase. A cazuela with más beef than mutón, carne choppeada para la dinner, un omelet pa' los Sábados, lentil pa' los Viernes, y algún pigeon como delicacy especial pa' los Domingos, consumían tres cuarers de su income. El resto lo employaba en una coat de broadcloth y en soketes de velvetín pa' los holidays, with sus slippers pa' combinar, while los otros días de la semana él cut a figura de los más finos cloths.[10]

Scores of other writers, from Richard Wright's *Native Son* (1940) to Gary Shteyngart's *Absurdistan* (2006)—, employ these jargons. When looked with an open mind, Ynglish, Ebonics (also called Black English), Spanglish, Chinglish, and other derivations are *not* bastardized versions of American English. They are American English.

The fact that writers use them in their narratives is the prerogative of American literature: it is its own authority.

3. In Defense of Ignorance

Talking about authority in American literature, my favorite literary critic is Edmund Wilson: learned yet not aloof (at least to me), he wrote essays on the nation's literature with such acumen

---

[9] Zora Neale Hurston, *Their Eyes Were Watching God* (New York: Harper, 1998).
[10] Ilan Stavans, *Spanglish: The Making of a New American Language* (New York: Harper, 2003).

and determination they contributed to giving the tradition the gravitas it has.

In *The Triple Thinkers* (1952), Wilson wrote that "one can never read the book that the author originally wrote, and one can never read the same book twice."[11] The sentence uses a thin veil to announce what reception theory takes to convey: that the literary experience is personal and therefore irrevocably framed in a specific time and place.

The best readers of literature are translators. They come as close to a text as the author. In fact, they may come even closer, finding crevices the author might not see.

The second best readers are literary critics. They take the time to understand a *text* in its *context*. The fact that these two words are related highlights the value of such a reading.

The problem is that in America no one gives a damn what critics say. The overall disposition toward them is more extreme: they are perceived as fussy, finicky, and doctrinaire. This is because, at its root, the nation thrives in being fervently anti-intellectual.

Yes, America is allergic to thinking and touchy about sounding serious. It loves inanity and mindlessness. Only scholars think (when they do). But why should they?

The Founding Fathers were all thinkers yet people prefer to see them as action figures. The same goes for the early American writers. Washington Irving, for instance, wrote eloquent biographical explorations of Spanish icons, Christopher Columbus among them. But he isn't seen (when he is seen at all) as a champion of ideas. What readers remember him for is for a parable called "Rip

---

[11] Edmund Wilson, *The Triple Thinkers* (New York and Oxford: Oxford University Press, 1952).

van Winkle" about the collision between personal and historical time. The character is a bozo: he falls asleep, which in America is the biggest sin. When he wakes up, everything is no longer the same. Suddenly, he has become a freak.

Critics are freaks because thinking takes time and no one has any time to waste in America. It is a solipsistic exercise, done alone, away from the hysteria of regular life. For that reason, it is seen with suspicion, as a sign of awkwardness, as a form of unsociability. And to think about literature is the most anti-social of all dilettante activities. A waste of time *and* money. Isn't literature meant to entertain, that is, to make people forget?

The rejection of intelligence in America, and the refusal to see thinking about literature, has forced book lovers to take refuge in campuses. This is a shame. Writers who support themselves through teaching end up generating a disdain for society. Their perception of the university as a safe haven turns it into a bubble. Those inside think of themselves as intelligent and those outside as idiots.

Some critics engage in close readings while others are interested in the ideological dimensions of a work of art. In the American academy, the pervasiveness of jargon (often coming from obfuscating French theoreticians like Michael Foucault and Jacques Derrida) has contributed to the perception that literary criticism is redundant.

It isn't. There is no literature without criticism, since it explains its purposes and elucidates its meaning. Yet not only French theory turns academic critics into inadvertent comedians. Other literary scholars who think of themselves as more accessible end up being equally lofty.

For instance, in *The Music of What Happens: Poems, Poets, Critics* (1988) Helen Vendler, a Harvard professor and the doyenne of literary critics interested in American poetry, states that the aim of criticism "is not primarily to reveal the *meaning* of an art work or disclose (or argue for or against) the ideological *values* of an art work." Vendler adds: "The aim of an aesthetic criticism is to *describe* the art work in such a way that it cannot be confused with any other art work (not an easy task), and to *infer* from its elements the aesthetic that might generate this unique configuration."[12]

To value a work of art? To infer from its elements the aesthetics it presupposes? To me, the whole effort sounds misanthropic. Why do such strange things if success is measured through profit and profit is always material?

It doesn't help that Vendler and her peers distill an outright disdain for pop culture. They believe a rigorous education is done away from the messy world out there on the streets. That education requires silence, contemplation, and maturity. This makes them look at mass art as cheap, transient, inconsequential.

I once talked to Vendler about the act—and art—of teaching. I wasn't surprised to find out she dislikes Socrates and his didactic method. She finds it anarchic, undisciplined. Teaching, she made the case, ought to be about the passing of knowledge from those in the know to those in the know-not. It should not be about exploring, through discussion, how the know-nots come to appreciate that truth is found through decantation.

---

[12] Helen Vendler, *The Music of What Happens: Poems, Poets, Critics* (Cambridge, Mass.: Harvard University Press, 1988).

Critics like Vendler see themselves as fountain of erudition. With erudition comes power. And any doubt about that erudition is perceived as a threat.

That is also the impression one gets from reading Harold Bloom. His disquisitions on Shakespeare (he wrote short volumes on a number of plays), Milton, William Blake, the Hebrew bible, and what he proposed was the anxiety of influence between poets of different generations, aren't a pleasure to read. The style of these books is muddy and uninviting. They aren't written for readers but for elucidators.

The opposite is true of Susan Sontag. Not that she wasn't pedantic. But she did something other seldom dare to do: she went from literature to other artistic endeavors, becoming a cultural commentator, which is different. Her essays on the suffering of others, photography, the function of war, and an array of other topics remain insightful.

Indeed, Sontag almost feels like a non-American intellectual. Aware of the nation's anti-intellectualism, she took refuge in other countries: France, the former Yugoslavia, Spain, etc. She was a public intellectual in the European and Latin American tradition, testing power without reservations.

In *At the Same Time* (2007), Sontag wrote: "The likelihood that your acts of resistance cannot stop the injustice does not exempt you from acting in what you sincerely and reflectively hold to be the best interests of your community."[13] She envisioned the purpose of critical thinking as a mechanism to investigate the structures of power in the world.

---

[13] Susan Sontag, *At the Same Time: Essays and Speeches* (New York: Farrar, Straus, and Giroux, 2007).

Other critics—Lionel Trilling, Alfred Kazin, Irving Howe, and James Wood, among them—take different approaches. And scholars like James Shapiro know how to write beautifully learned books that are also accessible to the general public. But again, to a large extent their craft is trapped in an echo chamber. Unfortunately, academic jargon is defended tooth and nail.

4. The Part about Superheroes

This is an important part. It deals with the least attractive kind of literature from the perspective of high-brow critics. Yet it's one that is stunningly popular, even when considering the country's general disdain for literature.

Call it genre lit. It gives readers what they expect instead of teaching them to expect something unique. In America, that line of writing is incredibly successful.

Different types include detective fiction, sci-fi, romance, horror, chick lit, dystopian novels, and even comics describing superhero adventures. I am a fan of all of them.

I like them not only for what they say and how they say it. I mainly like them because they exist; that is, they are a genuine expression of people's interests. Most readers don't want to know about Ulysses' homebound journey to Ithaca. Or about Proust's longing for his mother's goodnight kisses.

Edmund Wilson dismissed detective novels as preposterous. (I still like him!) In 1945, he published in *The New Yorker* an essay called "Who Cares Who Killed Roger Ackroyd?" Naturally, he was bombarded with a deluge of letters. And he was wrong, too. His view that only "serious" literature mattered was, well, unnatural.

"Serious" is a dangerous adjective. What is known as the Great American Novel—for instance, *Infinite Jest* (1996) by David Foster Wallace, who had a penchant for seeing himself as the most intelligent person in the room and whose work was meant for a reader just like him, Joycean, inspired by American arcana—was perpetually imagined under that sign: to be high-brow meant to be all-encompassing. But all-encompassing is a foolish dream. Literature isn't reality itself. You can't fill a glass with water and call it the ocean.

I don't want to sound pompous. In fact, I believe the profusion of genres in American literature is a sign of health. It is also proof of its pluralism. Despite the disdain from the establishment toward these genres (personified by Wilson et al.) the ubiquity of American pop culture has forced publishers to take a second look.

It is not accidental that thrillers and detective fiction are such staples of American literature—they might be the most popular of all genres. In their essence, these formulaic traditions are about the negotiation between order and chaos. They are also about rational minds called to organize the world methodically.

The father of American detective fiction is Edgar Allan Poe. His ancestry reaches back to the method of deductive logic promoted in the Middle Ages by philosopher William of Occam. Since the universe is ruled by cause and effect, no action—particularly no human action—is ever disconnected. Those connections tie it to a series of steps that, with the right frame of mind, are able to be inferred.

As an intellectual weaver, Poe is endlessly intriguing. In *Studies in Classic American Literature* (1922), D. H. Lawrence states:

> Poe had experienced the ecstasies of extreme spiritual love. And he wanted those ecstasies and nothing but those ecstasies. He wanted that great gratification, the sense of flowing, the sense of unison,

the sense of heightening of life. He had experience this gratification. He was told on every hand that this ecstasy of spiritual, nervous love was the greatest thing in life, was life itself. And he had tried it for himself, he knew that for him it *was* life itself. So he wanted it. And he *would have* it. He set up his will against the whole of the limitations of nature.[14]

American detective fiction then took a turn, disregarding Poe's legacy. Dashiell Hammett and Raymond Chandler, among others, targeted reason mercilessly. For them the attraction is in the rough-and-tumble ways in which the detective, not known for moral tidiness, gets caught in the dirt and corruption of a world run amok by subterranean forces.

Poe is also the father of horror—or at least its most illustrious American precursor, along with H. P. Lovecraft, who seems to me inferior—and of science fiction. His stories deal with monsters, hypnosis, mesmeric phenomena, and other extreme human behavior.

There is nothing puzzling about the fecundity of sci-fi in America. After all, this is a nation obsessed with progress no matter what the cost for it might be. But sci-fi does not always have the "sci" in it. Philip K. Dick, for instance, created peculiar alternative universes that are part futuristic (in the optimist sense) and part dystopian. It also feels as if his fiction was the product of an LSD trip. Or of a schizophrenic episode.

That is the case of *The Man in the High Castle* (1962). It looks at the United States as if Adolf Hitler had not lost the Second World War. On the contrary, in Dick's imagining the Nazis rule America with a mighty fist.

[14] D. H. Lawrence, *Studies in Classic American Literature* (New York: Penguin Classics, 1990).

Indeed, there is a peculiar fraternity between science and American literature. It seldom serves as a tool to educate the masses in scientific knowledge because that knowledge has become to such a degree obtuse that making it palatable to the public is a challenge. When such enterprise is achieved, marketers call it a work of scientific dissemination.

In the dystopian mode, Sinclair Lewis's *It Can't Happen Here* (1935) and Philip Roth's *The Plot against America* (2004) take a similar approach. The fact that both of them were "serious" writers made their books appealing to a non-genre-driven readership.

The work of Ursula Le Guin, on the other hand, verges more toward fantasy, though with equal political prowess. Indeed, her work is remarkable in its analysis of social mores. For what is sci-fi if not a detour to alternative realities while really talking about the present?

Le Guin was acutely aware of how sci-fi is seen by dull readers. She linked this attitude to the misconceptions around the pursuit of high-brow literature. In her curiously philosophical book *The Ones Who Walk Away from Omelas* (1973), she states that "the trouble is that we have a bad habit, encouraged by pedants and sophisticates, of considering happiness as something rather stupid. Only pain is intellectual, only evil interesting. This is the treason of the artist; a refusal to admit the banality of evil and the terrible boredom of pain."[15]

Le Guin believed in the existence of dragons. "People who deny the existence of dragons are often eaten by dragons. From within."[16]

---

[15] Ursula Le Guin, *The Ones Who Walk Away from Omelas* (New York: Harper Perennial, 2017).

[16] Ursula Le Guin, *The Wave in the Mind: Talks and Essays on the Writer, the Reader and the Imagination* (Portland, Oregon: Shambhala, 2004).

All these literary artifacts showcase the degree to which the popular core of American literature is, in essence, gothic. By this I mean violent, destructive, and melodramatic, a literature of darkness.

Contrary to common assumption, science fiction doesn't thrive *everywhere* in the world. It is limited to societies in which science and technology have such deep roots, the entire *Weltanschauung* depends on them. This is the case of Europe and Russia. It has also taken root in Asia, although with a different profile. But in Africa and Latin America, it is a marginal genre, if it is one at all.

Sci-fi in America takes center stage. This isn't puzzling. With its dizzying obsession with progress, the future is always in people's mind. Yesterday is easy to ignore. Today is malleable. But tomorrow—ah, tomorrow offers infinite possibilities.

Is the over-indulgence in genre literature in America—Stephen King is among the country's most popular authors ever—a sign of the nation never having gone beyond adolescence? Prudish critics insist on describing this passion that way, looking at its aesthetic value as "secondary," by which they mean superficial. (Graham Greene used to refer to thrillers as aperitifs.)

This dismissive look is obviously unviable, in part because of the larger-than-life role pop culture plays in the country's daily affairs. These secondary genres regularly come back with a vengeance, reassessing the way the mainstream looks at itself. For instance, people think of themselves as detectives, even if they have never been trained as such. There are more detectives on American TV and literature combined than in real life.

However, there is no doubt one aspect of genre lit is the penchant for melodrama. It thrives in raw, overstated emotions. People love that quality. It makes them feel understood.

I come now to the part on superheroes. I am the first to recognize that inserting such a section in a book on American literature might feel anachronistic. Yet that is the point.

Aquaman, the Avengers, Batman, Captain America, Hulk, Superman and Superwoman, Spiderman, Thor, Wolverine, and dozens of others—superheroes are an American invention, a concoction of the twentieth century ("the American century") through the tools of pulp culture.

There are white, Black, Latino, and Asian superheroes. Straight and gay. Human and androids. Beautiful and monstrous. Overconfident and humble. Made of steel and made of doubt. The diversity of American society is represented in the superhero mythology, which, in its complexity, rivals the pantheon of Greek deities and demiurges.

Superheroes serve a political and psychological purpose. They are endowed with supernatural qualities to defend humankind from all sorts of predators, which is exactly is how America sees itself in the world.

In what way are they a literary artifact?

True, they aren't packaged in full-length narratives the way a novel, a play, or an epic poem are. They are episodic. And they have multiple creators, meaning they are the byproduct of a collective endeavor.

In that sense, their presentation doesn't follow the format of Western art: individualized, defined by contradictions both internal and external, and expressing a particular aesthetic view. Plus, as works of art they fail to move their audience, though they surely get them pumped up.

All this is true. But these arguments fail to see the larger issue: like the travails of Zeus, Aphrodite, Apollo, Poseidon, and other gods, the drama they enact—the love affairs they engage in, the failures that result from them, the vulnerabilities that are exposed—is a soap opera of immense interest to the general public.

Indeed, American superheroes, in my estimation, are characters of an eternally recyclable *telenovela*.

The answer is simple: if graphic novels like Art Spiegelman's *Maus* (1991), in which Jews, Nazis, and Poles during the Holocaust are portrayed, though a postmodern technique, as mice, cats, and pigs—that is, a "serious" topic is analyzed by means of what used to be called "the funnies," then the funnies themselves (e.g., comic books) need to be approached more seriously.

Those comic books are formulaic. They depend on easy-to-handle polarities: a protagonist paired with a nemesis, a plot to destroy the planet, semi-divine powers, and so on.

America has turned superheroes into an industry, in literature as well as the movies. Its target aren't only children. Adults are enthusiastic fans.

Through these characters—as Michael Chabon made clear in his novel *The Amazing Adventures of Kavalier & Clay* (2000)—America's DNA reaches the world. Millions learn in them the narrative patterns of the journey of the hero. They also have access to literacy. And they are subliminally taught a moral code.

Indeed, the great contribution of American civilization is the erasure of the artificial division between the high- and low-brow.

5. Auto-Corrected

"Can I be spermed?" a student asked in an email last year, requesting to forgo an extra assignment. I laughed. At the bottom of the message, it read: "Sent from my iPhone." In less than five minutes, the student wrote back. "Apologies, Prof. It wasn't me but A-C. I really meant 'spared'." And she added: "It won't happy again."

This time I just smiled.

The complications brought on by technology are countless. And in them, the opportunities for Freudian slips never stop. Are we in charge, or has a coup d'état taken place, leaving the id in full control? Is the maxim "I don't know what I mean until I see what I say" still true when we usually forgo the opportunity to reread what we typed?

Needless to say, in the academy students aren't the only ones falling into this imbroglio. I do too, all the time. A week ago after class, I was asked by someone what I meant by the text "Yes, go ahead and festoon." What did I mean, indeed? (By the way, there's a website called Crazy Things Parents TEXT.)

My email exchanges with students are frequent. I encourage them to write to me after class with lingering comments on the material. I also ask them to shape their arguments for the final project through an e-dialogue. Sometimes the message I send them back is as long as 2,000 words. More often, it is telegraphic: "Meet me at 3:30pm," "Brilliant!," and "Your draft, I'm afraid, is as flat as a pita."

These messages might originate from my iPad, the use of which allows me to think a bit longer than when I respond from my iPhone, where sloppiness is more likely to prevail. Still, what matters, I tell myself, is that I'm in communication with them. That to me is why teaching is such pleasure: because I witness the making of a thinking mind and, to some degree, I'm responsible for it.

I'm supposed to be the students' guide. I have authority bestowed upon me to improve their language, to push them to new heights. In doing so, I sharpen my own mental processes, too.

But a phantom has inserted itself into our daily life: the Corrector. It is meant to speed things up when in truth it causes havoc. Before a word is fully spelled, the phantom guesses our intention, finishing it in front of our eyes. A mere second is required to confirm the right spelling ... but who has a second to spare?

The funny thing is that the phantom, in the Apple kingdom, is known as "auto-correct." (That's what my student meant by A-C.) Auto-correct, I take it, is synonymous with self-correct. It is the sender who is in control, even though the phantom, like a poltergeist, is doing the work. But are auto- and self- really the same thing here? And do we need such police inside our iPhones? Have we surrendered our liberty to the device? Do we need to be second-guessed? Some people don't buy iPhones for this very reason: outside Apple, they have more linguistic control.

And will the time come when the Corrector is available in oral communication? Well, that orality is already a fact, as one can dictate, not type, a text message.

Usually, when a student lets the Corrector take over, I ignore it—and I hope the same happens in the opposite direction. Or else, I play along. For instance, not long ago a Spanish-language student, after receiving an assignment prompt, replied to me: "*Vale, estic d'acord amb tu ;).*"

Mmmm...Inscrutable! Because *vale* is used in Spain as *OK*, I assumed he was in agreement with me and simply disregarded the rest. But then I decided to respond in gibberish, on purpose: "*Lind a stú....*"

I was proud to have usurped the role of the Corrector, choosing to be equally clumsy. My next thought was that, should this exchange continue, the two of us would be creating an entirely new language. Yet I stopped. Education is built on communication:

intelligible, decipherable, and logical. I told myself that the gestation of an alternative, maybe parallel code should be left for another—a special—occasion.

Then again, the phantom might be part of a cohort of darker forces. For one thing, I can't forget the statement "Can I be spermed?" Assuming, as one should, that the student typed "Can I be spared?," the corrector would have changed it to—what? Sperm isn't a verb in English; that is, auto-correct wouldn't choose "spermed" as a replacement for "spared."

Have our iPhones embraced dyslexia? Anyway, I'm glad it won't happy again.

Addendum: A few days ago, I was part of a three-way email conversation with two colleagues, both women, one an editor at Norton, the other a professor at UCLA. They had been pondering some scheduling issue and wanted my response, but I was busy all day delivering a series of lectures in a studio. Finally having time to reply, I meant to send a message that said, "Sorry, I've been taping all day." Except that my dyslexic device (or I myself?), instead of *taping*, wrote *raping*. I didn't realize it until one of them asked, "Ilan, did you mean taping?" and, within minutes, the other wondered, "I thought you meant rapping." I was embarrassed. Maybe I should have written *napping*.

All this to say that it is fascinating to see how technology changes language. For starters, our ABC seems to have changed dramatically before our very eyes and no one is making a fuss.

Not that it would matter.

It used to be that the alphabet was a sequence of twenty-six letters, from A to Z. The letter A came first for reasons that are arbitrary. Other than historical loyalty, there is no explanation—neither phonetic nor graphic—why it is at the beginning. The *aleph* in Hebrew starts the alphabet, and other Middle Eastern alphabets, such as the Phoenician, also had similar-sounding letters opening their writing systems. The B, the *bet* in Hebrew, could have led the pack, but it ended up second.

Looked at in toto, the list of twenty-six letters in the Roman alphabet is beautiful yet haphazard: A, B, C, D, E, F, G, H, I, J, K, L, M, N, O, P, Q, R, S, T, U, V, W, X, Y, Z, and not M, I, F, W, T, Z, Y, H, B, K, C, O, V, R, Q, L, U, S, E, A, X, N, D, G, J, P or any other arrangement you please.

Digital technology has made that sequence obsolete. Proof of it is the awkwardness with which the average teenager experiences a printed dictionary. He looks at it with utter amazement. Asked to find anything spelled with a W, paralysis takes over. Look up the word *chameleon*? He looks under K, then in C, until he connects C and H. The word *phosphorescent*? He starts with F. This strategy comes from sounding letters and is only tangential to my argument. But for these students, the fact that C is before K and F is before P is meaningless. That succession has been made irrelevant by technology. In online lexicons, C doesn't come before K; instead, the letters are concurrent.

By this I mean simultaneous, not chronological but synchronic. In the online version of *Merriam-Webster*, it matters little the order of letters. The key to locating a definition is knowing the first few letters of a word; the rest is done automatically by the search engine.

Grasping the idea of an alphabet that is simultaneous and not sequential is challenging to the mind because language is structured by a before and after. In the word *language*, L antecedes G, it doesn't coincide with it. It is as if in natural evolution, the transformation from a *Clepsydra* to a butterfly happened not gradually, in sequence, but all at the same time. Or if, in our understanding of history, the conquest of Mexico and Lincoln's delivery of the Gettysburg Address overlapped.

(Maybe they did....No doubt everything always happens in the present. The past exists because we have a way to refer to it, although not necessarily a verbal conjugation, since some languages don't have a past tense yet their speakers are capable of referring to events that occur before and after.)

The dictionary, in printed form, is an endangered species. I predict that it will cease to exist in the next few years. There is really no need for it, just as encyclopedias have no reason to exist as physical books; online resources have deemed them redundant. And with them will also go the concept of alphabetizing as a sequential, not as a concurrent, endeavor.

One could feel nostalgic about this transformation in cultural mores. Technology affects human behavior in subtle yet decisive ways. Reading time in traditional clocks made with a longer and shorter hand is troubling to adolescents; they prefer using ascending Arabic numbers. Likewise, organizing items with Roman numerals is cumbersome for them: finding Part IV, Proposition LVII, in Spinoza's *The Ethics* (*Ethica Ordine Geometrico Demonstrata*), which asserts that "the proud man delights in the company of flatterers and parasites, but hates the company of the high-minded," is harder than locating Part 4, Proposition 57.

Children today still memorize, in melodic form, their ABCs. In the future that effort is likely to remain intact, except that, for all it matters, they could learn it as BAC or any other random configuration.

Another sign of linguistic change in America is the contemporary use of ellipsis. To reflect on it, I need to offer an anecdote.

Some time ago, I was going over a draft of a graphic novel. It is called *Angelitos*,[17] and it is about a Mexican priest who devotes his life to protecting homeless children. I had written two versions, one in Spanish and the other in English, about a year ago. I had put them aside to simmer. When I looked at them again, I was struck by the abundance of ellipses in the two versions.

The protagonist is a passionate yet hesitating young man. In the dialogue I used the ellipses to convey his uncertainty. Now I had doubts about my strategy.

I realized, first, that the ellipsis is a relatively recent phenomenon (there are none in the Hebrew bible, for instance, although contemporary Hebrew does use them), and second, that different languages, verbal and numerical, use ellipses in different ways.

In Chinese, for instance, they are made of six dots divided into two subgroups of three, although sometimes, to shorten communication, people resort to only one subgroup. In mathematics the ellipsis can be used to mean "and so on," communicating the repetition of a pattern. And then there is literature, where the ellipsis often conveys omission, as in "The region of ... is full of unicorns."

In the two versions of *Angelitos*, my ellipses were consistent with Spanish usage. Called *puntos suspensivos* (suspension points) in Spanish, the device, as in French, implies doubt, is synonymous with et cetera, or suggests either silence or speechlessness.

In comparing the Spanish and English versions of *Angelitos*, it became clear to me that I didn't know to what extent English followed those rules. Since I have lived in the United States since

---

[17] Ilan Stavans and Santiago Cohen, *Angelitos* (Columbus, Ohio: Ohio University Press, 2015).

the mid-eighties, this discovery made me feel as if the road of assimilation, which has transformed me deeply as a person, is really never-ending. Although I'm a teacher, and have published a plethora of books—several of them translations—I had never stopped to think about the nuances of the meaning of the ellipsis in the two languages.

So I embarked on a comparative study.

What I found out was enlightening. According to the language historian Anne Toner, in her book *Ellipsis in English Literature: Signs of Omission*, the first appearance of the ellipsis in English dates back to 1588, in a translation by Maurice Kyffin of Terence's adaptation of the Greek play *Andria*.[18] She makes this point forcefully, but to me it seems like finding a needle in a haystack. Equally difficult to explain, other than blaming it on Darwinian evolution, is how, by the nineteenth century, the three little dots had become a fixture of the Queen's English.

The word "ellipsis" comes from Ancient Greek ἔλλειψις, *élleipsis*. In English nowadays, an ellipsis might appear in the beginning, middle, or end of a sentence. It can be preceded by a period or appear as four dots with added space between them. It shows up with spaces before and after the three dots or without them. The *MLA* and *Chicago Manual of Style* offer dissenting views on its usage. You may find it in parentheses or in between brackets. Its use is elastic: it might suggest further thought, condense a list or quotation, or simply mean blah-blah-blah.

It looks to me as if the biggest difference with Spanish is that in English the ellipsis doesn't connote doubt...or does it?

---

[18] Anne Toner, *Ellipsis in English Literature: Signs of Omission* (Cambridge: Cambridge University Press, 2017).

One of the most intriguing components of my study pertains to social media: in texting, the ellipsis is used to hold one's attention; that is, to announce that there's more to come, to politely change topics, or to stress anger, disagreement, or bewilderment.

And there are myriad ways of misusing ellipsis in texting. Some of these, it goes without saying, are a sign of the user's age. This was made irrevocably clear to me when my 20-year-old son, Isaiah (who goes by Zai), who studied at Kenyon College, told me that my texts are both too formal and too idiosyncratic.

To prove his point, he showed me an exchange between his friends Z and D: Z had just bought two tickets for a soccer game and invited D to the event. But D has more in her mind than a simple no: "are u comin" Z asked. "Maybe…" responded D. "You follow, Pa?" Zai asked. I said not quite. "Look, when texting you can use ellipses to mean a thought is unfinished. But people inject tone to that unfinishedness. In the example I showed you there is a difference between 'maybe' and 'maybe….' The former denotes doubt, even uncertainty: D is unsure of her schedule. The latter is a step further: D is withholding specific information. The 'maybe' is actually an 'I have something better to do.'"

Zai went on: "You, Pa, write a text that says, 'I need to think about it….' Nobody else texts that way anymore. It's enough to say 'I need to think about it' without even a period at the end because the period itself might entail anger. You only put an ellipsis if you're keeping something to yourself, some strategic information you don't want your correspondent to have. Get it?"

Well, sort of. Honestly, I was more confused than ever. Later, when I got back to the English version of *Angelitos*, every ellipsis, no matter its placement, suddenly seemed suspicious. There are stark differences between Spanish and English rules, I kept saying, but languages are by definition fluid, and rules are created to be broken.

Life is what happens outside an ellipsis. In any case, I ended up scratching out about 90 percent of the ellipses in the graphic novel, maybe more, in both the English and the Spanish versions. Why leave that much room to uncertainty, to speechlessness, to bewilderment?

Finally, I want to dissect the compulsive use by Donald Trump of exclamations marks. There are countless reasons to be outraged in the Trump era. This is just one of them.

Trump debases language all the time, in an off-the-cuff speech, via Twitter, in diplomatic correspondence, etc. His garbled syntax, his offensive adjectives ("Crooked Hilary," "Lyin' Ted"), the typos, the auto-correct blunders…I used to think W. was unsurpassable.

The debasement might be described as a deficiency. Trump's vocabulary isn't that of an adult but one more appropriate to a 12-year-old. He uses repetition and lacks discernment. But Trump shapes sentences in the form of turf, "we" vs. "them": we are right whereas they are corrupt; we are American and they are traitors.

I should qualify my argument by saying, first, that I'm an immigrant—and Mexican to boot. English isn't my language. I don't own it; I'm just a tenant in a rented house. Trump demonizes immigrants. However, immigrants are like converts: we love what we have because we know what it means not to have it. It's a love that makes us proud. Yes, I'm patriotic about English.

English isn't only my house; it is my home. I love its abundance, its cadences, its elasticity.

Yet—and here comes the second qualifier—I'm not a purist. Far from it: I'm in awe of how Cheryl the hair-salon owner, Josh the DJ, Edwin the X-ray technician joyfully articulate words every day. They don't destroy the language; they rebuild it. Dictionaries might tell them what's right and wrong but they can't stop them from shaping syntax in whatever darn way they please.

They aren't destructive in their approach; they don't debate English. Shakespeare, the verbal magician, would have appreciated their singular probity. Trump, in contrast, isn't creative in his verbosity. His bombast is cancerous. His intent is to trash everything around him unless it bows down to him.

Aside from immigrants, Trump stampedes against cities ("rat-infested"), against the media ("enemies of the people"), against diplomats ("Deep State mercenaries"), against Abu Bakr al-Baghdadi and his followers ("frightened puppies"), and against Speaker Pelosi (either a "third-grade" or "third-rate" politician) and Democrats in general ("un-American idiots"). He fancies high school recommendations to heads of state ("Don't be a tough guy! Don't be a fool!") and attacks truly successful entrepreneurs ("fake").

His intelligence, on the other hand, is "superior"; his phone calls are "just perfect." He is "the best president ever," including those who are—hopefully—still to come. Trump says all this with a straight face, without a hint of comedy. Does he even have a sense of humor?

The Founding Fathers knew the importance of English in the health of the Republic.

It isn't about rules. Trump isn't the only one who breaks them. "When I read some of the rules for speaking and writing the English language correctly," Henry David Thoreau wrote, "I think any fool can make a rule, and every fool will mind it."

It's about sensibility. Barack Obama, whom Trump fashions as his eternal antagonist, took pains to imagine the language of politics under a new light. His speeches, his impromptu reactions, his memoirs and interviews were cleanly delivered. I know it is proper for the pendulum to swing. But does it have to go this far?

True to his own nature, Trump has succeeded in surrounding himself with Roy-Cohn thugs, starting with mafioso Rudy Giuliani. There's not an iota of IQ left in the White House. This not only applies to domestic and foreign policy; it affects language, too. Not a single person in the cabinet is an inspired speaker. Mick Mulvaney, in press conferences, first confirming and then denying the quid pro quo with Ukraine, is proof. It was a "huge" travesty.

The president doesn't as much speak English as he suffocates it. His allergy toward globalism make him suspicious of anything international. He reminds me of Mencken, who said that "a living language is like a man suffering incessantly from small hemorrhages, and what it needs above all else is constant transactions of new blood from other tongues. The day the gates go up, that day it begins to die."

By the way, I like, and am thankful to, whistle-blowers. They aren't traitors. Instead, they are people who, forbidden to speak out, speak in instead. They communicate through silence and anonymity, a beautiful concept that highlights sound, truth, and morality.

These, then, are the extremes we have been forced to reach: the banality of narcissism fostering the irrelevance of meaning. Things are on the decline, though: Trump, in my eyes, looks more and more unstable every day, on the brink of a nervous breakdown. His speech is blurry, disgruntled; he barks, grunts, and howls. It is increasingly becoming impossible to make sense of what he says. I envision him in a strait jacket on his way to a mental institution that advertises the sign "Trump Hotel" at the entrance.

Language knows how to regulate itself. We don't need to wait for Elizabeth Warren or any other candidate of the Democratic Party to roll out a plan to resuscitate English back to life. As frightening as this moment is in history, it too shall pass, even if it passes like a kidney stone.

Fittingly, King Trump's epitaph will be a tweet tirade, full of misspellings and exclamation marks.

CHAPTER IV

SURVIVING DEMOCRACY

1. Books as Merchandise

As I mentioned in the previous chapter, in America, and also in its literature, the distinction between high- and low-brow is purely theoretical. In reality, the two exist in an incestuous relation—that is, if it can be said that such realms exist.

This is because even if in America what is good isn't popular and what is popular isn't good, sales are considered the bellwether of acceptance.

In *Minority Report* (1956), Mencken argues that "it is often argued that religion is valuable because it makes men good, but even if this were true it would not be a proof that religion is true. That would be an extension of pragmatism beyond endurance. Santa Claus makes children good in precisely the same way, and yet no one would argue seriously that the fact proves his existence. The defense of religion is full of such logical imbecilities. The theologians, taking one with another, are adept logicians, but every now and then they have to resort to sophistries so obvious that their whole case takes on an air of the ridiculous. Even the most logical religion starts out with patently false assumptions. It is often argued in support of this or that one that men are so devoted to it that they are willing to die for it. That is as silly as the Santa Claus proof. Other men are just as devoted to manifestly false religions, and just as willing to die for them. Every theologian spends a large part of his time and energy trying to prove that religions for which multitudes of honest men have fought and died are false, wicked, and against God."[1]

There is, obviously, the counter side: those that look down at the downtrodden. They believe literature ought to be a dignified endeavor, lofty and aloof. This is a literature emptied of any sort of ideology, although in so doing they infuse another kind of politics: detached, about the manners of the upper crust. At least in part, that wing is attached to an idealized Britain as a model, not only in social mores but in cadence.

Henry James is a prime case. His novels are webs of syntax. They delve into the life of expats in Europe, especially in England. They are about an elite that exists in a bubble: isolated, enamored with its own reflection. James is anything but apple pie: his are the landscapes of privilege without a hint of vertigo.

Closer to home, there are the two Johns, Cheever and Updike, and the cohort of suburbanites in an endless drive for boredom symptomatized in pools of alcohol and the excitement of extramarital affairs and other sexual adventures. This literature is also performative but in an altogether different way: about habits and gesticulations, about pretense, about the snobbishness that comes with power and the power that comes from loftiness.

Although my sympathies are clear, I shouldn't paint the dichotomy in such broad strokes. It doesn't have to be an either/or. There is much between these two approaches. At the very least there's confusion between them if not also cross-fertilization. America

---

[1] H. L. Menchen, *Minority Report* (Boston: Houghton Mifflin, 1956).

is pluralistic, meaning it has a plurality of viewpoints. William James, *Writings, 1902–1910*: "For pluralism, all that we are required to admit as the constitution of reality is what we ourselves find empirically realized in every minimum of finite life. Briefly it is this, that nothing real is absolutely simple, that every smallest bit of experience is a *multum in parvo* plurally related, that each relation is one aspect, character, or function, way of its being taken, or way of its taking something else."

Richard Rodriguez, for instance. In *Hunger of Memory* (1982), he explores his own limited resources as a child of Mexican immigrants to California. Poverty is a handicap. It blinds you. And it travels with you. But Rodriguez dislikes what the system does with him when it "tokenizes" his ordeal. No sooner is his intelligence spotted than he is taken out of the ghetto and moved to the land of the gifted. He receives applause and, along with it, scholarships and other forms of praise. The result is perplexing. He loses touch with his Mexican roots. He forgets Spanish while polishing his refined English. The consequence is inevitable: he becomes rootless.

No wonder he feels manipulated. The American rich, uncomfortable with their status, look for ways to express their sanctimony. One of them is lifting a handful of prize-winning "colored students" out of their habitat. They clone them: they dress them in the latest fashion, they wine and dine them, and they give them a brand new vocabulary. The effort establishes a system of patronage. It gives them an aura of good will. Those who have been refashioned are overwhelmed with a sense of unauthenticity. They have become fakes, deceivers, impostors.

There is Chang-Rae Lee depicting Koreans in search of place in America and Jhumpa Lahiri—in a Jamesian mode—looking for Indian identity.

This faction is about self-reliance. And the mother of self-reliance is Ayn Rand.

American identity is complicated. It is never a fait accompli. Instead, it is a conversation. Samuel Johnson argued that "As a question becomes more complicated and involved, and extends to a greater number of relations, disagreement of opinion will always be multiplied, not because we are irrational, but because we are finite beings, furnished with different kinds of knowledge, exerting different degrees of attention, one discovering consequences which escape another, none taking in the whole concatenation of causes and effects, and most comprehending but a very small part; each comparing what he observes with a different criterion, and each referring it to a different purpose. Where, then, is the wonder, that they, who see only a small part, should judge erroneously of the whole? or that they, who see different and dissimilar parts, should judge differently from each other?"[2]

The questions that arise are clear-cut. Who reads American literature in the United States? It used to be a healthy middle-class interested in its own condition. It used to be an eager public that felt part of the conversation. The empire was on its ascent. It had gravitas. It had capital to spare. But that audience is fractured now. It is much more divided. Or forced. There are students assigned books, especially the classics, who engage in reading like robots:

---

[2] Samuel Johnson, "The Adventurer," *The Works of Samuel Johnson*, vol. 3.

the seek help from summaries and other tools to digest plots and reduce character to a handful of lines.

There are book clubs, hundreds of them. Most of them are unintellectual, that is, middle-brow. Few of them are daring. For the most part, they are built around comfort zones and proven tastes. No big adventures in terms of assignment because they might disappoint. And disappointment is un-American.

There are also the specialists. A whole industry is built around particular classics in order to keep them on track. And there are the author's fan base. Fan literature is the most profitable. Writers write to please their followers. They train them to expect a certain diet and then feed them that diet to exhaustion. That's what the publishing industry does: it gives the audience what it wants. It doesn't encourage readers to want anything different. This is ironic because difference is the promise of American literature: let us be different, let us be ourselves.

Does this sanctimony explain why a bestseller sells an average of twelve thousand in a country of 325 million?

And do these books reflect the diversity of opinions in American life?

If there is a metaphor for America, it is that of the market place. The nation sees itself as a space where people gather to sell and buy merchandise.

This places the focus on capital.

Success is a synonym of accumulation. To have is to possess. Everything is capital: time is capital, place is capital, experience is capital, relationships are capital, emotions are capital. Success is also control: to have is to shape, to arrange, to dispose.

Defeat, on the other hand, is about attrition. To be out of control is to lose.

There is an in-between though. Deliberate renunciation of capital—from emotions to material possessions—is considered a form of elevation.

Arguably the most contested type of capital in America is memory. To remember is to be connected; to forget is to be adrift.

In American literature, longevity is about memory. The sought-after objective is to be remembered. In the short run, that is achieved through publicity. But immortality is about being remembered beyond the present, for the present is ephemeral and nothing scares America more than what is transient, replaceable, nondurable.

Yet memory in American literature is invariably portrayed as a trap. Since it cannot be controlled, it is always contested. Generations subsist by manipulating memory, by cutting it to fit their needs.

Regardless of their high or low quality, books in America are merchandise. They exist to be acquired—that is, to belong to individual readers.

Should books be sold? I frequently ask people this question, in part because I want to inform myself but also because I am ambivalent. I love books. I live and die by them. But I find myself buying fewer and fewer. And I know I am not the only one. The book industry is in crisis.

In my view, we are witnessing the end of "the book era." What lies ahead? A different understanding of what that artifact is. Dictionaries today still define a book as "a written or printed work consisting of pages glued or sewn together along one side and bound in covers." Needless to say, no one takes that definition seriously.

And yet, we still have books: different kinds of books, books that don't look like books, books that behave like anything but books. People aren't consuming them, at least not the way they used to. Would it make sense to make books available with advertisements? Would that change the nature of the game?

A time of crisis is a time of reckoning: we should ask questions and look for answers.

Let's start by acknowledging the obvious: literature is a business. As an author, I make my living through it. The sale of books sustains not only us but a larger battalion of people, from editors to translators, from publicists to marketers—and publishers, too.

For it is no secret that the book industry—in the United States, at least—is in deep trouble. Supply is far bigger than demand. The number of books released annually is on the ascent while the number of buyers is on the descent. Is there a way to reverse this trend? Is it that the book as a conduit of storytelling is dying out, or might the problem be with the concept of selling books?

Books were not always perceived as a mass-market commodity. That view is relatively recent: it dates back to the Enlightenment, with the advent of industrial capitalism, when intellectual property and the idea of authors as sources of wisdom and entertainment became commonplace.

Homer, the ultimate classic and an ever-attractive commodity among publishers, isn't an author, as there is no proof such a person existed. Instead, Homer is a stand-in to describe an oral tradition about the Trojan War and the return of Odysseus to Ithaca. At some point in history, that tradition was fixed in hexameters on a page and passed down to us now. Who owns those hexameters? The Greek people. Or, more broadly, Western civilization. Or, since that concept is contested today, I should say *every* reader who partakes in Homer's narrative.

Yes, the reader as owner. Naturally, this isn't an attractive idea for publishers. They like to think of themselves as caretakers of the classics. They release new editions of the *Iliad*, translating it anew to achieve a single objective: to make money. Yes, they might be altruistic, but the goal is always the same: profitability. In that sense, Homer isn't different from the Bible: anyone can make money out of it. The same goes for other classics in the public domain.

Contrary to common assumptions, a book in the public domain can be a valuable commodity. In fact, it is more valuable than most titles under copyright. The challenge is to make the classics alluring as merchandise.

Similarly, my intention here is to reflect on what makes books not only available to large audiences but also sellable and, as important, profitable. At least the first part of that is the dream of democracy: to disseminate information in egalitarian ways. Again, that dream is a relatively late development. Books didn't sell in large quantities in the Middle Ages, when they were mostly religious items in monasteries, although early examples of financial exchange, as Stephen Greenblatt and others have shown, date back to this epoch.

Market value became a fixture of the Enlightenment, as *Don Quixote* vividly shows: a 50-something hidalgo wastes his limited income on chivalric novels—an unproductive endeavor according to Cervantes's ironic narrator. Cervantes himself didn't make much money from book sales. Along the same lines, Shakespeare's quartos became marketable only after his death.

In short, books were not sold for most of their history. Mass production and sale is a new development. Not selling them isn't so inconceivable after all.

We have Johannes Gutenberg, and the invention of movable-type printing, to thank for giving birth to the age of the modern publisher as venture capitalist. Gutenberg is my hero even despite himself, since, for all intents and purposes, he didn't think his invention was directly linked with capitalism.

Nor did he portray himself as a promoter of democratic values. Instead, he was a practical man looking to solve an age-old challenge: how to make the printing process more agile, less cumbersome. His mechanical press made books an irreplaceable device, without which modernity is inconceivable.

A friend of mine often says that books are like food: they sell because people need to eat. True, we buy books because we hunger for information, for knowledge, for amusement. But in economic terms, books aren't like food: you really don't need them to survive. In fact, the need for them is dying out, at least in regard to the standard printed book, even though print is still approximately 70 percent of the market (if we talk about literature per se, the percentage is higher). Necessity is the mother of invention.

Books used to sell because people needed stories. They wanted new stories, stories that related to their lives. They also wanted to know about the past. And they were curious about the future. Books sold because humans are curious. But there are other means to satisfy that curiosity today, from TV to movies, from theater to the internet. The discreet units of knowledge called meme (a caption, a photo, a video, doctored on its way to a recycled life) has become a favorite tool of language.[3]

---

[3] I'm fascinated by memes. The insistence with which they descend on me through an assortment of technological devices is overwhelming. I do my best to ignore them—but to no avail.

Not long ago, I took the opposite approach: I spent several days looking at thousands of memes I had inadvertently accumulated in my garbage file. They included videos where Hillary Clinton's lips pronounced words she never uttered. (Sounds familiar?) There were pictures of World Cup players being lampooned for missing a decisive penalty kick. (I already had trouble identifying them.) In one meme, a tweet was recalibrated to make me laugh about Mexican "*bad hombres*," but it upset me instead. And a press release about diversity from Starbucks was repositioned to announce a new coffee blend from Colombia designed to exonerate white people for their sins against humanity. In between, I came across numerous photoshopped pictures of public figures (film and TV stars, Washington politicians) in compromising sexual positions.

Time and again, I have thought about how vulgarity has become commonplace. But in part what actually interests me isn't the content but the very existence of these memes. What really is a meme, anyway? Could there be a science called "memetics," devoted to studying the mimetic activity of these small units of culture?

One person's waste is another person's treasure. Think of the discarded outtakes of a movie; or a symphony's unused sections; or the drafts a novelist destroys before a book assumes its final form.

Not that memes are art forms. Not yet. The power of a meme is found in its ephemeral nature.

My interest in them requires some background. Years ago, I became obsessed with selfies. I wanted to know the degree to which these instant self-portraits change us psychologically. Are we more narcissistic nowadays than at any time before the disposable cameras made by Kodak and Fuji came into existence? The more I thought of selfies, the easier it seemed to connect them with artists like Rembrandt, Vermeer, Van Gogh, Warhol, and Cindy Sherman. At its core, the history of self-portraiture is the history of humankind looking at itself in the mirror. That mirror is now an iPhone.

In collaboration with Nuyorican artist Adál, I ended up writing a book-long essay on selfies (other spellings: "cellphie" and "sellfie") called *I Love My Selfie* (2017). The conclusion I reached isn't that we are more narcissistic than our predecessors. It is just that there are more and faster ways to express that part of ourselves.

Memes are equally enthralling. The origin of the word is uncertain. In ancient Greek, mimesis means imitation. That's the function of art: to copy reality. This etymology is useful in that it points to artifacts as cultural capsules passing from one individual to another. A treatise by Aristotle, a poetic trope by Homer, a play by Sophocles are all such capsules. They have a producer and a recipient: the producer endows them with a message that is confined by a specific set of parameters; the recipient shares those parameters and thus is able to decode that message.

Books are in crisis today because they must compete against other, more tempting media. Hopefully, even as readership wanes, books will still be produced—because people will always hunger for this type of storytelling, for this type of private thinking process.

A printed book is a technological device. So is the iPad. Digital books have become attractive because they are easily transportable, because the reader is able to upload multiple stories on the same device, and because—*voilà*—they are affordable. However, the basic model of digital books is the same for printed books: a publisher puts one on sale and an interested reader buys it. If the book is appealing and—miracle of miracles!—lucky, it will sell well; if it isn't, it will disappear from sight.

Are there other business models through which stories might reach readers in book format? Let's think of different venues. I will start with commercial radio, Facebook, Twitter, and large segments of the internet: they reach consumers not by asking

---

To exist, a meme—like a selfie—must travel. The traveling of memes creates insiders and outsiders: The former are those in on the meaning; the latter are those deliberately left out. That is, the meme creates its own imagined community.

I recognize that this definition is too loose. However, I'm not frustrated by this openness because what's important isn't what a meme is but the life it leads, the impact it has, and the subtle ways in which it culturally transforms us all.

The young traffic with memes at astonishing speed. I see them creating memes, laughing at them, celebrating or condemning them. They see memes as democratic items. Through these memes, they proclaim their ideological loyalties, even when it feels as if those ideologies are hyper-sarcastic. They proclaim pop culture to be everyone's property: there is no private property, especially online; every theft is a type of appropriation.

This is unusual because, in our age, the concept of appropriation is highly contested. It is ironic that the young often protest when the narrative of a disenfranchised group is stolen. Yet to create memes, they steal left and right without an ounce of shame.

Anyway, all this is to say that my spam file has become an incredibly fertile site for a lover of semantics like me.

them to pay but through advertising. Users respond because they offer an attractive proposition: stories that allow people to feel connected. All one needs is a radio, an iPad, or a laptop. Who pays the bill? Advertisers.

TV functions in the same way. Instead of paying ABC, CBS, or NBC, viewers buy merchandise advertised in commercials. HBO, Showtime, and other cable channels have pushed the medium to another realm: subscription TV. These networks do use some forms of advertising in their programs, but it is solely used to promote their own products. Other networks such as AMC, which showcases *Mad Men*, among other series, combines subscription revenue with more traditional forms of advertising.

In contrast, public radio and TV for the most part depend neither on advertising nor on subscriptions but on individual and corporate donations. These are juxtaposed with a basic funding package coming from federal, state, and local budgets making possible the basic services of those public channels.

How about selling literature through subscription? Or through a mix of subscription and ads? Netflix and Spotify successfully combine the two. Could books be produced in ways to create the passion of *Game of Thrones*? This model, by the way, isn't that different from how Charles Dickens offered some of his meganovels in the second half of the nineteenth century: in serialized form, with chapters being released on a weekly basis in newspapers. Readers drawn to Dickens's plot and style regularly bought newspaper copies. Magazines also use this strategy.

Film presents the same model, although perhaps with more chance of success today. Blockbusters are produced in Hollywood by private production companies ready to spend lavishly on an assortment of genres to recoup their investment. Smaller movies have minuscule budgets whose sources come from private entities. At times the combination of these two formulas allows for a modest movie to become a "sleeper."

My point is that media thrives in a diversified market, one where manufacturing an item (a movie, a radio program, a cable mini-series) doesn't always depend on a single investor's deep pocket. In the book industry, cases abound of self-published titles where authors big and small, from Stephen King to debutants rejected by corporate editors, sidestep publishers in order to embark on the publishing adventure themselves.

As a society, we have already transformed—with considerable pain—our idea of a bookstore from a physical entity to a virtual one. Amazon.com is the principal provider. But here we face a substantial risk: the company has become a monopoly controlling not only prices but also business practices. On average, Amazon. com takes upwards of 30 percent of the price of every e-book sold, an amount that is lower than for print books, which is closer to 50 percent. This is roughly the same with Barnes & Noble. The company also forces the publisher not to sell the item at higher prices elsewhere. Plus, like other retailers, it doesn't allow advertising inside the books. Since the majority of readers nowadays consume books through Amazon.com, the company de facto legislates the market. It also controls our freedom to sell.

What if we wanted to place ads in books? Shouldn't we push the big transnational retailers to open up? What if instead of readers bearing the brunt, it was left to companies to place ads in books so that readers would get them directly and through the commercials compensate those companies with a profit? Or to sell them through weekly installments à la *Breaking Bad*? Interestingly, these days, a big part of the audience for these shows watches them online, bought from iTunes and such, without ads or a subscription. Could that be the route books take as well?

Granted, this idea of using ads in books sounds intrusive, even obnoxious. I myself hate it. I dislike watching commercial TV, in large part because of the ads. I'm a devoted NPR listener. Still, a good idea isn't only about the pleasure it provides but about the venues it opens. When I watch HBO and Showtime programs, I use the mute button in my remote control to mitigate the presence of ads. Surely it is possible to imagine a similar scenario with books. Aren't we able to do that with YouTube?

When I presented the model to some forty high-schoolers in Oxford with whom I spent a week reading the classics, their first thought was that I was a fool. I wanted them to visualize a copy of *Pride and Prejudice* with a Coca-Cola ad in the inside cover, a Victoria's Secret ad in the back, and maybe a series of smaller ads at the start of each new chapter.

The teenagers spoke to the intimacy they feel when reading and how it would be spoiled. I asked them if they don't feel intruded upon when watching *The Walking Dead*. No, they said. They've gotten used to the ads. So—I added—could you get used to ads in *Leaves of Grass*?

I showed the high-schoolers a paperback copy of *Fahrenheit 451* I happened to have with me: it featured an ad for other covers of books by Ray Bradbury as well as the publisher's website and, in the back matter, questions for reading clubs and a list of other world classics the reader might be interested in, from Arthur Koestler's *Darkness at Noon* to Margaret Atwood's *The Handmaid's Tale*. Aren't those ads also?

I tempted the kids to reflect on the type of subliminal product-placement advertising Hollywood has accustomed us to, as in the case of a James Bond movie filled with BMWs and Alfa Romeos. What if we allowed similar ads in novels? Truth is, we already do: authors have considered product-placement possibilities in their work as a form of revenue. The jury is still out when it comes to results, yet no one appears to be angry enough to refuse to buy a good read that endorses this model.

One of the most attractive, fastest-growing items in the digital publishing industry today is the "single." Singles are quick reads of between five thousand and thirty thousand words. One competitor even tells people the approximate number of minutes— between half an hour and 120 minutes—these nanobooks require. The model sells not only because the majority of people don't have time to read but also because they see reading as a chore. Interestingly, their price ranges from $1.99 to $2.99, which means profit is minuscule unless a vast quantity is sold. Thus, publishing large numbers of singles, books that require limited editorial labor, broadens the profit margin.

Like most full-length books, a vast number of singles sell only a couple of dozen copies. Should they be free, then? What if free singles were stuffed by the publisher with ads for other titles by the same author as well as other titles in general? Even better, what if instead of selling the single at $1.99 the item came with paid advertisements and was given away for free?

But why would Abercrombie pay for an ad in my copy of *On the Road*? Because it might reach a desirable segment of consumers, as it does with magazines, which, by the way, are also in a dire business. Readers of Kerouac are the audience the company depends on. That is the same reason corporations advertise on Facebook, Twitter, Instagram, and other social media: to create taste patterns, to invest in the mind, not only in the looks, of its clientele. Corporations aren't about profit as a route to branding. That is, they are about image.

Some small publishing houses such as Wave, Open Letter, and Ricochet are taking the subscription route seriously, albeit in the print, not necessarily the digital, world. These and other electronic-only ventures (like Frisch & Co.) and electronic-friendly publishers deserve attention, which means experimentation is taking place. Ugly Duckling Press, for instance, offers all its print titles online for free. Behind the strategy is the idea that fans will support writers by other means.

I am involved with Restless Books, a digital-publishing venture seeking to address the dire need English-language readers have for translations of world-class literature from around the world. One of its objectives is to make books—not only poetry but novels and nonfiction—available in two or more languages to readers everywhere.

And in Japan and South Korea, there are publishers releasing books on Twitter or stories designed especially for iPhones, not to mention the countless websites devoted to bringing books exclusively online. How do they make money? Through ads, donations, and, sometimes, plain charity.

It is important to keep in mind another route: the author as personality, making a living from speaking engagements. The crowd-sourcing events website Together is a fine example of how bookselling might look in the future. This begs a comparison with the music industry, where advocates for free music argue that more widely distributed titles would garner more fans for artists and thus higher attendance at concerts and sale of merchandise.

To conclude, my feeling is that the health of the publishing industry—or some semblance of it!—can only be sustained by a hybrid approach. The book as merchandise might not have an expiration date if we learn to see its marketability in a flexible fashion. Human curiosity is innate to our existence. But paying cash for an item isn't.

As long as we live in a capitalist system, books will always be sold, although the idea of what constitutes a book as well as what we understand as a sale are undergoing dramatic transformations. Decades ago, I had a theater teacher who lived by a single mantra: don't give the public what the public wants; instead, teach the public to want something different. If the public likes it, if it makes it feel satisfied, it will not notice the difference.

More than anything else, the American century was about fiction, perhaps because America permanently lives under the illusion of itself. While dreams are as old as civilization, fiction, the shaping of dreams into self-sufficient narratives, are relatively new. Myth isn't fiction and neither is folklore. Fiction is a byproduct of modernity: the creation of alternative universes that serve as reflections of one impossible defective one. And of all the vessels in which fiction presents itself, the novel is the most marketable. No wonder it is also the most American.

This marketability is found in its disdain for allegory. Allegory depends on symbols: a mask isn't a mask and a pitchfork a pitchfork. Fiction, on the other hand, is realistic. It wants to tell things as they are to a flaw. One of the gravest sins of authorship is said to be the embellishment of facts. The audience wants things plain and simple, without additives. Again, this makes it perfectly suited for America, the land where honesty, it is often repeated, is favored above all. Don't let others portray you as what you are not. That's the lesson John Proctor learns in Arthur Miller's *The Crucible* (1953): Be honest! Be yourself!

Not accidentally, Leslie A. Fiedler, in *Love and Death in the American Novel*, argues that "between the novel and America there are peculiar and intimate connections. A new literary form and a new society, their beginnings coincide with the beginnings of the modern era and, indeed, help to define it. We are living not only in the Age of America but also in the Age of the Novel, at the moment when the literature of a country without a first-rate verse epic or a memorable verse tragedy has become the model of half the world."

But novels aren't read anymore with any kind of fervor. It happens, occasionally, for young adults. But not adults. They are too unfazed. It used to be that when a new Saul Bellow title hit bookstores, readers rushed to stores. No more. The age of reading is in eclipse.

The demise is not of its own doing alone. Others have visibly matured as well and are now in command of the stage. The world is more global today than when Lawrence was dissecting Poe, Hawthorne, and Melville. But the true villain is the lack of interest in literature as a whole. Reading is an endangered endeavor. Why waste time flipping pages when a screen is able to vomit a plotline in less than two hours through beautifully executed images? Storytelling is as essential as ever. Without it we aren't humans any more. But stories now come in all sorts of easy-to-handle packages.

Globalism makes all part of a large family. Yet there's a lie at the core of this truism: a family is by definition small. You know your relatives. They make you feel safe and unique. Too large a family is no family at all. You're lost in a sea of sameness.

2. The Coolness of American Libraries

The history of American literature is the history of the nation's libraries. These have changed over time, from mere depositories of books meant for circulation where patrons, driven by taste and curiosity, replenish their intellectual needs, to sites where an assortment of community services are offered, especially for the disenfranchised. They offer internet services, English-language classes for immigrants, children's activities, job-hunting tools, and even Yoga.

In that sense, the American library is an essential ingredient in the nation's ongoing democratic conversation. Intellectual exchanges are orchestrated in them designed to propagate the semblance of community the nation needs, even in times of ideological fracture as in the Trump years.

Kurt Vonnegut, in *A Man without a Country* (2005), praised this function. "I want to congratulate librarians, not famous for their physical strength or their powerful political connections or their great wealth, who, all over this country, have staunchly resisted anti-democratic bullies who have tried to remove certain books from their shelves, and have refused to reveal to thought police the names of persons who have checked out those titles. So the America I loved still exists, if not in the White House or the Supreme Court or the Senate or the House of Representatives or the media. The America I love still exists at the front desks of our public libraries."[4]

I too celebrate this spirit. The challenge, however, is that the American library—out of need, no doubt—has pushed books

[4] Kurt Vonnegut, *A Man without a Country* (New York: Random House, 2005).

into the basement. I speak both concretely and metaphorically. In many branches, books are a second thought. The reason has to do with the technological move by the culture at larger from printed to digital books. Most new books are available as e-books. And classics are made free online.

What's then the purpose of shelving books for library patrons? They can access them anywhere they want.

At this point I could engage in a litany of why printed books matter more: the way they feel in front of one's eyes, how the experience of reading is different. But my purpose here isn't nostalgic. I want to talk about libraries.

However, I do want to talk about the dramatic diminution of reading as a habit. It is said that the average American reads one book a year. Yes, one single book a year! The thought is frightening, especially when one recognizes that to read is to think, to read is to imagine the world in an individualized way.

It isn't a new complaint. In one of Plato's dialogues, the *Symposium* (c.385–370 BCE), one of the participants grumbles that in Greece reading is a practice exclusive of those interested in philosophy, mathematics, and other pursuits of the mind. No similar complaint, at least not in those terms, recurred in the Middle Ages, when the degree of alphabetization was minimal. Monks and the ruling ecclesiastic elite were known to be the ones in charge—maybe it is better to say they were bestowed with the duty—of learning, in contrast with the peasantry, which was deliberately kept ignorant as a strategy of control.

It is known that after the first volume of *Don Quixote* was published, in 1605, the way people accessed it—at least people not part of the nobility—was through public readings in town plazas and other open spaces.

It is true that in contrast, books reach Americans in multiple ways these days, not only as e-books. They might arrive as audio books, in serialized form through online services, and so on. Likewise, book clubs have remained and even increased their popularity. Yet no matter how we see it, the act of reading is in decline.

As with everything else, in America readers vote with their wallets. Turning a book into a bestseller is a referendum not only about the quality of the volume itself (best-sellerdom might mean it is just trash) but about the audience that endorses it. For audiences are anything but homogenized. Each genre has its own following, as does each author and style. There are sophisticated readers and popular readers.

To become a fan of a literary figure is to turn the values the figure expounded into an ideology. Readers purchase t-shirts, tote bags, tote bags, and postcards to express their adoration. Such are the passions that fandom often results in tribalization: if you're one of us, you must be ready to adore our author without restrictions.

To the degree possible, libraries stay away from this kind of Balkanization. They want to be as comprehensive in their offerings as possible, even though some specialize in one particular type of literature their patrons might favor.

In any case, in a nation on steroids as a result of hyperstimulation, American literature is at a disadvantage in comparison with other forms of entertainment: TV, movies, the internet, video games, even radio. In American libraries, the sections on visual material have grown at a very rapid speed, sometimes far outpacing the standard book collections.

This goes hand in hand with the fact that in America people remember through popular culture. Otherwise, people no longer have individual memories. They now remember the past through the movies, the TV shows, and the streaming services they subscribe to. Remember the episode of *Star Trek* in the third season, in which the Enterprise is about to stop an asteroid from crashing with a Federation world only to discover that the asteroid is a Generation ship? I saw it when I was 7 years of age and my parents were in the middle of a divorce. Or the episode of *Gilligan's Island* called "Hair Today, Gone Tomorrow"? It was shortly before John Lennon met Yoko Ono. Memories don't have a life of their own. They are inevitably anchored though pop culture highlights.

No empire in history has been as adept at trafficking with culture as the United States. It thrives in creating a market, then satisfying it with all sorts of cheap merchandise. Not to be up-to-date in pop culture is to show one's age, to be behind the times. The bombardment of references is crucial in order to be *au currant*, which in turn makes you cool. That's the biggest trophy: coolness. To be cool is to be awesome.

As a concept, coolness comes from Black culture. It defines a type of fifties entertainment (a jazz musician, a fashion designer, a novelist) who, aware of the oppressiveness of the environment, created a cocoon of safeness by feigning remoteness. Ella Fitzgerald was cool. Dizzy Gillespie was too. (A similarly youth-specific, culturally savvy concept is woke. To be woke is to understand how cultural capital travels. It implies reading reality beyond the surface, appreciating the double entendres it throws at you.)

Countless American writers, from John Updike to Grace Paley, have a love affair with libraries. The majority come from middle-class backgrounds. For them the public library is a platform to alternative universes. These are three exaltations. First, Annie Proulx in her novel *Barkskins* (2016):

One reason for the [Port Townsend's arts-and-crafts Carnegie, allied with the Jefferson County Library]'s success is the town's population. A characteristic of Port Townsend is citizen involvement in hundreds of volunteer projects from maritime science to the kinetic sculpture race. The library is beloved and although there is a staff of more than 15 people what makes the place efficient and engaging are the more than 70 volunteers. But Ms. Eisler's personal commitment to libraries is more than her affection for the community. She believes and says "librarians live and die by First Amendment rights."[5]

Amy Tan in her memoir *Where the Past Begins* (2017):

My first library gave me the freedom to exist in private, to choose and even be greedy. I took 10 books the first time—illustrated books, fables, fairy tales and happy stories of white children and their kind parents. A week later, now initiated, I was allowed to walk to the library by myself, carrying the 10 books I had finished reading, knowing I could choose many more to furnish my vast secret room, my imagination, all mine.[6]

Finally, Barbara Kingsolver in her novel *Unsheltered* (2018):

Everywhere I've gone since, I've found libraries. Those of us launched from bare-bones schools in uncelebrated places will always find particular grace in a library, where the temple doors are thrown wide to all believers, regardless of pedigree. Nowadays I have the normal professional reliance on internet research, but my heart still belongs to the church of the original source. Every book I've written has some magic in it I found in physical stacks or archives.[7]

My own debt to the American Library is enormous. In Mexico, where I grew up, public libraries were always dysfunctional: they

---

[5] Annie Proulx, *Barkskins* (New York: Scribner, 2016).
[6] Amy Tan, *Where the Past Begins* (New York: Harper, 2017).
[7] Barbara Kingsolver, *Unsheltered* (New York: Harper, 2018).

were understaffed, the weekly schedule was irregular, books were stolen .... It was only when I came to the United States that I understood the centrality these institutions have.

While I travel, whenever I have some free time I spend it at the local public library. I let myself get lost in the shelves, wandering without any specific purpose. I always come across surprises. I also meet friends at these libraries. And plenty of strangers with whom I have insightful conversations.

In Wellfleet, Cape Cod, where I spend part of the year, the public library, right in downtown, has been an oasis during humid seasons. I found signed copies of Edmund Wilson's books in it. (He was a long-time resident of Wellfleet.) I have also read detective novels I would have never come across. And collections of essays.

Whenever I am in one of these places, I feel safe. I have an internal peace I seldom replicate anywhere else. The librarians eventually become my friends.

The underfunding and people's apathy toward reading are worrisome. Ray Bradbury once said that "You don't have to burn books to destroy a culture. Just get people to stop reading them." The quote comes from *Fahrenheit 451* (1953), which was written less than a decade after the Second World War and in the middle of the McCarthy era. Bradbury's novel is about the burning of books in a totalitarian state.[8]

In that foreseeable future, there will be no libraries. Fortunately, for now there are. John Steinbeck tells a starchy anecdote in *America and Americans* (1966): "Not long ago," he writes:

---

[8] Ray Bradbury, *Fahrenheit 451* (New York: Simon and Schuster, 2012). Francoise Truffaut, the French film director, adapted it into the screen. Bizarrely, Truffaut's version has aged in a unique way: the images have a retro quality difficult to explain.

after my last trip to Russia, I had a conversation with an American very eminent in the field of politics. I asked what he read, and he replied that he studied history, sociology, economics, and law.

'How about fiction—novels, plays, poetry?' I asked.

'No,' he said, 'I have never had time for them. There's so much else I have to read.'

I said, 'Sir, I have recently visited Russia for the third time and don't know how well I understand Russians; but I do know that if I only read Russian history I could not have had the access to Russian thinking I have had from reading Dostoevsky, Tolstoy, Chekhov, Pushkin, Turgenev, Sholokhov, and Ehrenburg. History only recounts, with some inaccuracy, what they did. The fiction tells, or tries to tell, why they did it and what they felt and were like when they did it.'

My friend nodded gravely. 'I hadn't thought of that,' he said. 'Yes, that might be so; I had always thought of fiction as opposed to fact.'

Steinbeck adds: "But in considering the American past, how poor we would be in information without *Huckleberry Finn*, *An American Tragedy*, *Winesburg, Ohio*, *Main Street*, *The Great Gatsby*, and *As I Lay Dying*."[9]

Very poor, indeed.

3. Teaching in the Age of Intolerance

American literature starts and ends in the classroom. It starts there because whoever is a writer-to-be is likely to discover the magic of

[9] John Steinbeck, *America and Americans and Selected Nonfiction*, edited by Jackson J. Benson and Susan Shillinglaw (New York: Penguin Classics, 2003).

literature as an assignment, or else in response to the tedium that comes from feeling disengaged with the educational purpose.

And it ends in the classroom because, at a time of precipitous decline of the reading habit, books have their largest audiences among students enrolled in this or that course.

Reading for pleasure is one thing and another altogether different thing is being obligated to read. The latter has a pernicious effect. It might traumatize readers who on their own are unlikely to find pleasure in the artfulness of a book. There is nothing worse than a teacher forcing a student to read. Unless you write a report, you will blah-blah-blah.

I myself was an apathetic reader when I was young. I didn't quite feel repulsion for books but the emotions I experienced weren't far from it. The duty to read for a class made me dislike any interesting book that came my way.

Until things changed. Why and how I can't quite explain. As I remember, it happened around 17 or 18. From one day to the next I was an avid reader. I have never looked back.

When I was young I also never thought of myself as a teacher. Why would anyone want to spend most of their life indoors with a bunch of rowdy kids? Yet I can't think of anything more rewarding than teaching. Or more challenging.

I'm a professor at a small Liberal Arts college in New England but I don't like the word "professor." It is too snobbish. I also don't like the word "academic." It makes me feel isolated, detached.

I prefer to be called a teacher. I didn't set out to become one. In some ways, I became a teacher out of necessity. I'm an immigrant from Mexico. I needed a visa. Teaching seemed like a worthy route to getting one.

I teach literature not only to college students. I also teach Shakespeare in prisons. I teach in public libraries to a population that is truly diverse. I teach in senior facilities. And in the summer, I teach middle- and high-schoolers. I love books. My mission is to make students love them as well. I open them in front of their eyes. Not just any book, but what I call "tested books" by writers of all backgrounds—Whitman, Dickinson, Melville, Hawthorne, Saul Bellow, Baldwin, Paley, Nabokov, Bashevis Singer, Toni Morrison, Henry and Philip Roth—that have survived the passing of time. In other words, the classics.

I particular enjoy teaching the classics. I love the fact that as an immigrant, I get to introduce Americans (most of my students have been born in the United States) to the literary tradition that defines them. I approach these books as an outsider who has entered the banquet. I do so by choice.

Teaching American literature is a contested endeavor. Obviously, it is all about representation: who gets to tell the story of the nation and in what way that story is told. Since the past is never settled, neither is literature. This means that the reaction a new crop of students is going to have to a book I have taught numerous times is likely to surprise me. It might even unsettle me.

No wonder the classics are under siege. They are seen as biased, dubious, and suspect. I tell students that classics are books we don't only read but reread. That is, they have to survive scrutiny, which is no easy feat.

As I see it, there is nothing wrong with rejecting the classics. The transmission of knowledge shouldn't be mechanical. Each of us needs to discover a classic afresh because the classics were not written for abstract readers. They were written specifically for *us*. If we don't like them, we should read other classics.

Ours is an age of intolerance that really doesn't value books. Washington is the land of distrust. The nation has recently been commanded by a Latin America-styled tyrant who not only doesn't read (the book he wrote was concocted by someone else) but whose lexicon seems to consist of 750 words. To a large portion of the country, difference is a threat.

In our own community, the disease of intolerance is present. Before the presidential election, racist and anti-Semitic graffiti appeared on Mount Tom. Likewise, anti-immigrant, xenophobic, sexist, and misogynistic incidents have been reported in our public schools.

Prejudice doesn't live outside campuses only. Liberals, who fashion themselves as free of bigotry, can be just as chauvinistic. Opposing views that are considered unwelcome are shut down. Students of the current generation—the cool, distracted millennials—are imbued with preconceived ideas that are equally narrow-minded.

The whole brew is toxic. Truth is frowned upon. Nothing matters because nothing lasts. All of which makes teaching more important than ever.

The classroom cannot be divorced from the real world, even when that world is in a state of disarray, as is ours. Each classroom must be a testing ground where ideas are pondered thoroughly. It must also be the place where we slow down. In the classroom, we must take stock. Yes, there ought to be debates, but it is useless if those debates are screaming matches or based on dismissive attitudes. The classroom must lead by example.

In the current climate, Updike and Bellow are out. (Dead white men talking meanly about women!) Dickinson is an eternal source of love. (She's mysterious. Plus, in the eyes of students her poems are mercifully short.) Adrienne Rich's feminist voice is strident. Junot Díaz, the most aesthetically ambitious Latino writer of his generation, was accused of disrespecting women. Likewise, Langston Hughes's closeted homosexuality is perceived to be a problem, unless it might be argued that it was a strategy of self-defense.

Along these lines, not long ago I had a Latino student who looked down at anything a white person said because, she said angrily, it was "biased with privilege." Her position was understandable. She came from a neighborhood in Los Angeles where interaction with non-Latinos was minimal. Montaigne once said that "we call barbarous anything that is contrary to our own habits." It was only after the class engaged with other kinds of difference that the student felt more at home.

To me, the classroom is where we fine-tune our better selves. It is where we discover what we don't know and where we question everything. Doubt rules in the classroom because doubt is the door to knowledge. And knowledge must be won. Nothing should be taken for granted.

Especially any text that binds us, including the U.S. constitution. If there is anything that will serve as social glue, it has to be thoroughly interrogated.[10]

---

[10] I asked in the preface, "American Carnage," if the American constitution better served in the dumpster. The majority of nations in the globe don't have one. And those that do don't turn it into a fetish.

I'm not a constitutional lawyer, although at times I have wished I were, studying its minutia the way rabbinical scholars explore the Talmud. The constitution represents a venerable tradition, yet, like any thinking lay person, I'm concerned about its far-reaching power.

Since its framers were slave-owners interested in perpetuating their own capital, since the Second Amendment allows for the ownership of weapons to protect against whatever they understood as lawlessness, and since women weren't consulted about their own reproduction rights....In other words, the document is biased. Better to have a code of laws that apply to current circumstances. And stop using a capital "C," for heaven's sake. The constitution is no more sacred than the bible.

All these long-held thoughts meandered in my mind after I attended a performance of Heidi Schreck's Broadway play *What the Constitution Means to Me* (2019). Actually, more than a play, this one-woman show (though at different points there are a couple of other actors on stage) is an excuse to debate the durability of the 1879 "supreme" law, originally comprised of seven articles delineating the parameters of the country's government.

"We the people of the United States, in order to form a more perfect union"....In the span of an hour and a half, Schreck recreates her teenage self in debates she participated in, locally (she is from Wenatchee, Washington) and nationally, about the pros and cons of the constitution. As she does it, she comments on her present-day feelings toward the views of that younger self. She won several of those contests, eventually using the money to pay for college. Nevertheless, today she is ambivalent about her once gung-ho arguments. The *we* in "We the people" is still an exclusive (e.g., non-inclusive) club.

Would it have been better if the framers of the constitution had created a nation without such a text? Israel doesn't have one; instead, it has a series of Basic Laws. Argentina, depending on how one defines it, has had a total of seven constitutions, the most recent dating to 1994. Does it matter? This proves that nations cannot exist without laws but they surely can without an "inalienable" constitution.

By the end of Schreck's play, she has discussed Supreme Court justices laughably misunderstanding the issues of the day. She has argued that the constitution, rather than a living document, has been used as a shield against change. And she has repeatedly stated that the conception of what a citizen was at the end of the nineteenth century is somewhat different from now. What she means is that the constitution allowed those who made it to perpetuate themselves in power.

The audience is then invited to ponder: keep the constitution or dump it? Should we have a new one that reflects our modern aspirations as citizens?

In the performance I attended—my son Isaiah and I sat next to Meryl Streep and Emma Thompson—the public was encouraged to take sides. Since then, Isaiah and I have continued the conversation. He thinks the question "Should the constitution be dumped?" doesn't prompt a yes or a no. The response should be the study of the words *within* the constitution itself.

I agree with him fully. We all need to know what the U.S. constitution does to us in order for us to know what we can do to it. I want the document to be adjusted to the needs of society. I also want it to reign "supreme." The word is important to me. Having seven constitutions in the span of a couple of centuries,

Words uttered in the classroom must be made to matter; they must be listened to fully and patiently, not only for what they mean but for how they sound: their music, their rhythm. Likewise, the classroom is where silence must be given its due. I love the sound a student makes before words come out and when thought is still being processed. There is a hiatus, a pause. That pause is the seed of wisdom.

And what about the teacher? In my view, the teacher is a companion, like Virgil in the *Divine Comedy*. An authority, yes, but not authoritarian. And certainly not a know-it-all.

Teaching is what anchors me. It has been more than twenty-five years since I started doing it. I wouldn't give up a single minute of it. But it goes without saying that teaching today is a battered and embittered career. Teachers are blamed for all sorts of ailments: reading failure, low test scores, poor academic performance.

---

the way Argentina has done, frightens me, making their code of law too mercurial. Likewise having basic laws, as Israel has.

The doctrine of Originalism, expounded by Justices Antonin Scalia and others, resists the concept that the constitution in always mutating. All living codes must, since change is the one constant of our universe. Who cares what the framers of our constitution meant when they wrote it? What matters is how the law is interpreted in a specific time and space.

Imagine, for a second, that the bible had never been written. Its stories, its policies, its theology would still exist in the form of oral tradition, what in Judaism is known as *Torah she-be'al-peh*. Would there be a Western Civilization? Surely not since that civilization, contested as it might be, is textual. That is, it exists because we all converge on the same written text. Having stories, policies, and a theology printed on a page fixes the content while allowing it to be transformed in the act of transmission.

It is important to remember that those who drafted the constitution were part of the *we*. They endorsed slavery yet slavery is an abomination. The same goes for ownership of weapons by any citizen who fancies them. Or depriving women of their reproductive rights. Attitudes such as these belong to another epoch. We are more reasonable.

In sum, the U.S. constitution is imperfect yet perfectable.

The result is that teaching isn't often an attractive option for our undergraduates.

Yet teaching, I say this with *absolute* certainty, is an essential endeavor, again particularly when it comes to the endeavor of bringing literature to the attention of the next generation. It is about honoring who we are. The classroom is where intellectual curiosity is at home, where our cultural values are shaped. It is where people think, individually as well as in group. For that reason, it is crucial that we again make teaching the revered, humble vocation it used to be.

As our nation goes through this rough, ugly period, hopefully one that will pass soon, the classroom is where humanity starts.

4. Born Translated

My intention in this section is to reflect on translation in American literature. Already some preliminary thoughts have been planted, as when I discussed Henry Wadsworth Longfellow's influential rendition of Dante's *The Divine Comedy*, highlighting the degree to which, released shortly after the American Civil War, and impacted by the death of Longfellow's own son, it allowed readers, and the author as well, at a time of intense loss, a channel with which to establish a dialogue with their own dearly departed.

A classic is a book whose value is heightened with the passing of time. A book that is better on a second reading and a third and a forth . . . . A book that isn't timely but timeless. A classic is a book that chooses its readers rather than the other way around. A book that accumulates readings. A book in which we have a conversation not only with our contemporaries but with readers that came before and readers that will come after. Mark Twain once said that a classic is also a book that no one reads but everyone knows. And Borges believed that a classic is a book capable of creating a nation.

There is a particular affinity in American literature for acknowledging the influence of the literary classics.

In fact, translating the classics in America is a sport. It didn't come out of the blue. The activity was inherited from the British, the owners of a long tradition in translation, which until the mid-twentieth century was mostly focused on European titles. There are multiple versions of dozens of them, from Dostoyevsky's *Crime and Punishment* to Kafka's *The Metamorphosis*. Often the translators are scholars although on occasion they are also novelists, playwrights, and poets.

This sport is money-driven. The classics aren't only perennial; they are also in the public domain. The incentive inspires voracious publishers interested in selling thousands of copies annually without paying any royalties. It isn't a zero-sum game: the endorsement of one title doesn't represent the detriment of another. Instead, it is more like a Darwinian universe: some classics thrive as the fittest in the camp because of a variety of factors while others go out of fashion, the current generation of readers letting them go as non-pertinent.

In America, reading of the classics is considered an entryway to a set of values that make individuals useful, engaged, knowledgeable citizens. Yet reading—especially the classics—is always a checked activity: it is done by a few, mainly for instructional purposes. And the question is: whose values are being endorsed by the classics?

For starters, these are books about imperfect characters. Gregor Samsa isn't really an epigone of moral rectitude, or at least in the way Kafka describes him. He is just like the rest of us, struggling with our own demons and even succumbing to them.

In the age of relativism, there is also the discussion of whose code of morals the classics ought to be endorsing. In a world increasingly defined by diversity, the canon of classics in America remains stubbornly European, although dents have been made to expand the shelf. The values are therefore mostly from the places traditionally seen as bastions of civilization: England, France, Germany, Russia, Spain, and Italy.

Either way, although the endeavor of reading the classics is perennially diagnosed as being in decline, they continue to be required reading in American universities. For better or worse (though mostly for the better!), it is in the classroom where most Americans discover them, forced—or else, persuaded—by teachers of their enduring value. This introduction is like an alarm clock: it wakes up new talent to the world's literary reservoir.

Now I want to take an altogether different approach to translation, one fitting with the general theme of this chapter: democracy and literature.

America is a nation with little patience for translation. Only a small elite—mostly made up of academics—is interested in the nuances of translation. The vast majority of the population believes English is not only the dominant language in the country but also the only one that truly matters in the world.

"Three percent" is the proverbially infamous number often referred in the world's publishing industry to the minuscule fraction of books translated into English on an annual basis. Like the Stock Exchange, the percentage fluctuates somewhat, though seldom as drastically as to unexpectedly change the landscape. It is forever stuck in the lowest digits. Other languages put a generous amount of time, energy, and resources to translate books into their cultures: in Germany, it is 58 percent of the annual titles that come from other parts of the world, in France 47 percent, in Spain 42 percent, and so on.

Historically, the number has been steady also. During the colonial period, translations from French, German, Russian, and to a lesser extent Italian were regular fixtures in the American reader's diet, although, with the publishing industry still in its cradle in the emerging nation, books in small numbers were imported from England. To various degrees, George Washington, Thomas Jefferson, and other Founding Fathers were passionate readers. When he died, Washington had a copy of *Don Quixote* not far from his bed.

The American publishing industry expanded visibly in the nineteenth century, but, again, consumption of foreign literature was limited to an educated elite. Emerson, Whitman, Beecher Stowe, Hawthorne, Melville, Dickinson, Poe, and other writers were all followers of European literature.

The reasons for the pernicious "3 percent" are symptomatic. It all starts with the allergy to foreign languages in America. In a country of immigrants, English reigns as king. Assimilation starts with speaking English, no matter how broken. There is also the fact that Americans see themselves as the epicenter of the world. Why translate from other cultures if nothing ever really happens there? Hollywood, TV, music, fashion, cuisine, and the internet set the tone—no matter where you are, if you aren't tuned into American culture, you just aren't tuned in.

Consequently, American books—available already in airports and other transit areas in remote corners of the planet—are the most translated in the planet; that is, far more of them travel outward to other languages than those arriving home from different linguistic habitats. This not only helps sustain American culture, and American English per se as the prevailing lingua franca, but creates a never-ending financial bonanza.

American literature is born to sell. Unlike other countries where writers are conduits of rebellion, in America they are entertainers. Whatever political clout Sontag, Naomi Klein, Rebecca Skolnik, and others might have, they parade it from within the marketing stage. Only rarely does an American writer end up in prison.

In America, the loss of salability translates into true exile.

Aware of their one-way street translation appeal, American writers look at their audience globally, even when they write about local themes. They take the versatility of American culture as a privilege, assuming that translation must be automatic. If a book is successful, it must not only be reviewed in the *New York Times* book pages but be translated rather quickly into as many tongues as possible. (Writers in other linguistic habitats—German, French, Spanish, Italian—also have this attitude. Yet they don't assume, like American writers do, that this is their God-given prize.)

The effects of translatability are enormous. In *Born Translated: The Contemporary Novel in the Age of World Literature* (2015), Rebecca L. Walkowitz states that "Many novels do not simply appear in translation. They have been written for translation from the start."[11] To design a novel *for* translation assumes that America is ground zero: what happens in it happens globally.

There are various ways to translate. One might be either loyal or disloyal to the original, enhancing it at every turn. (Might a

---

[11] Rebecca L. Walkowitz, *Born Translated: The Contemporary Novel in the Age of World Literature* (New York: Columbia University Press, 2015).

translation actually be better than the original?) And one might try to be historically accurate or not.

Some examples. When translating into English a seventeenth-century Spanish *comedia* like Pedro Calderón de la Barca's *Life Is a Dream*, it is possible to use contemporary language to modernize the somewhat archaic material. The effect of that strategy is to bring the text to the present. The opposite is also possible: to use archaic language to bring back today's reader to Calderón's time and place. The two strategies are equally valid. They only differ in intention.

In a market-driven economy, most translators of classics embrace the first strategy. They look at the second as an academic exercise.

And when it comes to a literary work recently published, there are also divergent approaches. One is to be as literal as possible, hoping to convey in minute detail the author's intention. That strategy, in my mind, gives too much credit to the author, who is indeed the creator of the work. Yet once that work is published, what matters is not what the author wants but what the reader needs—from the translator's viewpoint.

In contrast, a translator might remain as close as is feasible to the original while embracing the full panoply of poetic possibilities of the target language. In other words, creativity is required, albeit in small quantities.

I'm of the opinion that there is a specific kind of truth for translators. They must be trustworthy while also being somewhat disloyal.

In my work as publisher, I see these attitudes first-hand. On occasion, a novel might even be launched simultaneously in the English original and in the various translations, creating what is known as "a total moment." This is the drive behind best-sellerdom: to have readers tune into a book everywhere at the same time.

American literature is like McDonald's fast food: cheap prices, everywhere the same. In *Democracy in America*, Tocqueville had already reached this conclusion. "By and large the literature of a democracy will never exhibit the order, regularity, skill, and art characteristic of aristocratic literature," he said. He added that the formal qualities would be neglected or even despised:

> The style will often be strange, incorrect, overburdened, and loose, and almost always strong and bold. Writers will be more anxious to work quickly than to perfect details. Short works will be commoner than long books, wit than erudition, imagination than depth. There will be a rude and untutored vigor of thought with great variety and singular fecundity. Authors will strive to astonish more than to please, and to stir passions rather than to charm taste.[12]

I'm not sure it is the right conclusion. Writers work at various speeds, whether they are in a democracy or in another type of system. Their patience and dedication have to do with their inner clocks. Yes, they react to their environment. But artists are known to resist that environment no matter what.

It is true that a reward-driven nation like America fosters a regime of rapid, often careless production. But that regime has also given place to unqualified masterpieces whose global impact is unquestionable.

---

[12] Alexis de Tocqueville, *Democracy in America* (New York: Library of America, 2004).

In any case, I empathize with the concept of "born translated." The late-stage capitalism we inhabit allows the market to erase borders—or at least, to ignore them—in ways Robert Frost would have applauded (if he hadn't been such a crank).

5. Unhappy People

In 1923, D. H. Lawrence, fresh off the scandal of *Women in Love*, wrote a short nonfiction book called *Studies in Classic American Literature*. With the explosion of great literature in the nineteenth century, it was, among other things, a clarion call for American writers to fully assess their role as nation-building intellectual leaders in what was called "the American century." "Listen to the States asserting," Lawrence writes. "'The hour has struck! Americans shall be Americans. The U.S.A. is now grown up artistically. It is time we ceased to hang on the skirts of Europe .... All right, Americans, let's see you set about it. Go on then, let the precious cat out of the bag. If you're sure he's in."

The cat was indeed let loose. But living outside the bag isn't easy.

Over a decade after Lawrence's call for maturity, Langston Hughes, in his poem "Let America Be America Again" (1935), first published in the magazine *Esquire*, wondered if early in that century the American Dream was for all Americans. "(America never was America for me)," he stated, ghettoizing the sentence, variations of which appear throughout the poem, in parenthesis. That is, America displays its full colors only by eclipsing some of them. In doing so, Hughes questioned Lawrence's invitation: excuse me but *for whom* has the hour struck?

America, the creator of Disneyland, is a hedonistic nation. Its principal purpose is the illusion of making people happy.

Yet the emperor's new clothes are invisible. The Covid-19 pandemic has awakened the country to its deep-seated unhappiness.

The #MeToo Movement has made visible the misogynistic undercurrent that has defined America since the start. Women are objectivized, demeaned, abused. Likewise, Black Lives Matter, with roots not only in the Civil Rights era but in rebellions dating as far back as 1739, has put the spotlight on institutionalized racism. Police brutality is a daily occurrence targeting Blacks and Latinos. The government is mostly run by old white men with little connection to the overall population. At the same time, political correctness is corrosive, reducing people to their physical features: you are your skin color, your gender, your economic strata, your religion. This is sheer reductionism. One of the disasters of the Trump era has been the obsession with whiteness; white is privileged; white is nearsighted; white is indulgent. And while on the surface diversity is championed, the truth is that the opposite of white is Black. Very little space is given to Latinos, Asians, Native Americans, and so on. This is a nation trapped in either/ors.

Hope remains, though. Actually, in America hope is always in the air. And Hughes's poetry explores that aspiration. He showcases the extent to which American literature is a conversation. With Whitman, for example. Hughes, the polymath of the Harlem Renaissance, dares to turn himself into a Whitmanian cosmos: "I am the young man, full of strength and hope,/ Tangled in that ancient endless chain/ Of profit, power, gain, of grab the land!" Where are you, grandfather of splendid visions? he seems to ask. Why haven't the dreams of yesteryear become realities for all?

In what way has America stumbled? What happened to freedom? Who controls the free?

Yet in spite of everything, Hughes is convinced opportunity remains real in America, equality still in the air we breathe. "O, let America be America again—/ The land that never has been yet—/ And yet must be—the land where *every* man is free./ The land that's mine—the poor man's, Indian's, Negro's, ME—."[13]

Distress is only one side of the American literature, though. There is also happiness, often presented in infectious ways. And gullibility, like Singer's "Gimpel the Fool."

Gullibility is the attribute of credulity. Americans tend to think of themselves as happy people because they believe in all sorts of things. True things as well as untrue. This credulity keeps them focused in creating a myth of themselves.

For instance, that America is mighty and that, as Ayn Rand proposes in *Atlas Shrugged* (1957), in order to achieve that mightiness, it is crucial to foster a race of self-reliant individuals, entities whose mind is polished into existence, so to speak. Rand argues that such a characteristic is crucial in a capitalist society:

> Do not let your fire go out, spark by irreplaceable spark in the hopeless swamps of the not-quite, the not-yet, and the not-at-all. Do not let the hero in your soul perish in lonely frustration for the

---

[13] Langston Hughes, "Let America Be America Again," *The Collected Poems of Langston Hughes* (New York: Alfred A. Knopf, 1994). I find Hughes's poetry stunningly powerful. Whitman was indeed his model and Harlem his residence, although he traveled to the Caribbean and the Soviet Union. His connection with Cuban writers like Nicolás Guillén, and the aesthetic debt he incurred to Pablo Neruda, infuse Hughes with a Latin American quality.

life you deserved and have never been able to reach. The world you desire can be won. It exists...it is real...it is possible...it's yours.[14]

Although that national self-reliance might lead other nations to imitate it, they will never achieve a similar feat. For America is unlike anyone else.

It is a convenient delusion, obviously. But what is literature if not delusion? As the turmoil of 2020 ravages a nation in need of self-definition, the clues to that reckoning are in its books. F. Scott Fitzgerald, in *This Side of Paradise* (1920), says that "in literature, your longings are universal," that "you are not lonely and isolated from anyone."

In literature, Fitzgerald states, "you belong."[15]

---

[14] Ayn Rand, *Atlas Shrugged* (New York: Signet, 1996). Less a literary figure than an ideologue, Rand is a polarizing figure whose oeuvre has turned her into a darling of conservative thinkers. Their investment in her is as promoter of individualism and self-reliance.

[15] F. Scott Fitzgerald, *This Side of Paradise* (New York: Martin Lewis, 2020).

THE SECOND AMERICAN CIVIL WAR

A Reckoning

Dear Editor of the *Daily Hampshire Gazette*:

How ironic that we are now bringing down Antifa monuments eulogizing soldiers that valiantly fought in the Second American Civil War (2023–7). During the Trump years, effigies of Confederate lieutenants and colonels were either destroyed or relocated into store rooms in museums. It felt like a fever: the nation as a whole needed to categorically reject the false promises of Reconstruction.

Those who championed change were themselves turned into statues. And look at us now: beheading the beheaders. I guess Allen Ginsberg was right: sooner or later, one witnesses the frying of the best minds of our generation, all shamelessly destroyed by madness.

Does anyone remember in America any more the roots of this bloody war? This is indeed a nation of amnesiacs.

The statue of Lieutenant Sergio Meléndez was brought down in Amherst, Mass., in the middle of the night, on May 25, the anniversary of the death of George Floyd in Minneapolis, a victim of police brutality. Why was it done with such fear?

As we commemorate yet another anniversary of the Battle of Palmer, Mass., in which almost 200,000 people died in the span of three days, I can't but be overwhelmed by shame. Two of my daughters died in battles in Virginia and Arizona. I'm part Korean. Their mothers were Colombian and Vietnamese, respectively. I keep telling myself: all of this could have been prevented.

Not that yesterday's ceremony—in which President Gupta consecrated the grounds by time and again invoking the 272 words Abraham Lincoln used at Gettysburg in 1863—was unworthy. Your editorial insinuates that much (*Daily Hampshire Gazette*, April 7, 2031). Yet you're unhappy with President Gupta's use of the term "coexist," and you bring her to task for it. "We cohere," you write, "and we coalesce. But coexisting is no longer enough!"

You might be right. The Second American Civil War has clearly not put Humpty Dumpty back together again. Nearly 3 million dead in the span of less than five years. In comparison, only about 620,000 soldiers died in the First American Civil War (1861–5). The origins of the two conflicts are summarized in a single word: color. Was the optimism upon which our country was built utterly misconstrued? Were our original sins irrevocable? Is it still possible for a citizenry whose origins are all over the planet to truly coalesce in peace?

Everyone blames the Trump years. They were toxic, no doubt. It is universally known that, after he won the November 8, 2016, election, the entire world entered a period of stagnation. It was as if time were moving backwards. In the United States, a considerable segment of the population marched against Trump. "Not My President!" was a favorite slogan.

The divide was irreconcilable. The left and the right had long stopped being civil. A bumper sticker now at the Smithsonian reads: "Elect a clown, expect a circus." Before Trump came to the White House, he already had made a career as a buffoon. He had no principles. He was incapable of sustaining a coherent ideological view. He was dangerously impatient. Trump's language was made to be advertised. In fact, more than a president, Trump was a marketer: he sold a portion of the electorate a bill of goods.

Shakespeare's *Julius Caesar* was insistently staged in those years. Audiences were looking at an interpretation of the play that fit their anxieties. It is no coincidence that in Act II, Scene 1, Brutus wonders: "How many times shall Caesar bleed in sport."

Indeed, this Roman play became the blueprint of what was to come. Sedition, as everyone knows, was in the air. It didn't come from the usual suspects: the pro-cosmopolitanism crowd. This sector was also guilty of follies. Not of treason. That came from Trump's entourage, as your newspaper, and others, fittingly reported. Like Brutus, Cassius, Casca, Trebonius, and other conspirators, those surrounding Trump had egos to feed. Not as huge as Caesar's but large nonetheless.

I remember reading a book by Professor James Shapiro of Columbia University, a specialist on the Bard—he had written an insightful volume on 1606, "the year of Lear"—called *Shakespeare in a Divided America* (2020). The results of the November 3rd presidential election were a foregone conclusion. Joe Biden was the winner of the Electoral Vote as well as the popular vote, hitting over 80 million votes.

Professor Shapiro devoted a chapter to the Abraham Lincoln assassination. Throughout his life, President Lincoln was a frequent reciter of Shakespeare's plays. His introduction to them was William Scott's popular *Lessons in Elocution*. In his later years, he attended numerous takes on Shakespeare's plays in

Washington, D.C. John Wilkes Booth, his assassin, was, like his father and brother (although with considerably lesser talent), a Shakespearean actor. A fervent Confederate, he used *Julius Caesar* as a blueprint, not only to find in himself the gumption but to orchestrate the steps that led to the fateful moment, on April 15, 1865, when, in his eyes, tyranny would die.

Booth told a friend that of all Shakespeare's characters he liked Brutus the best (excepting only Lear). That friend—I will never forget—later said that Booth's "study of and meditation upon those characters had much to do with shaping that mental condition which induced his murder of President Lincoln," losing "his identity in the delirious fancy that he was enacting the role of Brutus and that Lincoln was his Julius Caesar.

Somehow it was as if Shakespeare himself had been implicated in the President's Lincoln's demise. I say this because we Americans are individualistic to the core. During the Covid-19 pandemic, scores of Americans refused to wear masks because in their eyes they infringed on their personal freedom. Yet we are less free than we think. In fact, larger-than-life forces constantly determine who we are and how we act. I don't mean exclusively economic, political, and religious forces. I also mean stories. We are characters in stories. We ourselves tell these stories but more often than not we are characters in someone else's story.

The stories might be contemporary. They might also be ancestral. Shakespeare and other illustrious writers captured the essences of those stories in their work. Regardless of how much we resist, we are condemned to repeat those stories—in perpetuity.

Your editorial is correct. Neither Trump nor Pence, Castro, or Piltowsky are the cause of our cosmic tragedy. It wasn't the fault of Russia. Or ISIS [Islamic State of Iraq and Syria]. Or Lieutenant

Menchaka. It was our fault—and ours, alone. The irrationality that befell us has no name. Look at China today. Look at superpower Chile.

Just as the twentieth century saw the rise of America, the twenty-first witnessed its unraveling—and rather precipitously. F. Scott Fitzgerald once said: "There are no second acts in American lives." The same goes for reckless empires.

Is it at all surprising that we have gone through this Second American Civil War when for decades the National Rifle Association made it infuriatingly easy to acquire semi-automatic weapons? In the end, it wasn't about self-protection, as advocates kept on suggesting. It was about building militias whose sole mission was to enhance particular ideological views. It is a well-known truth that war is the continuation of politics by other means. But America had forgotten that war is also a crime.

What about the demonization of immigrants and the inhumane repeal of DACA [Deferred Action for Childhood Arrivals]? Or of Blacks, Jews, LGBTQ, and other "deviants"? Sooner or later, the rhetoric of hatred became a tool of destruction. Americans forgot that words aren't made of air.

And what about the biblical flood brought along by Hurricane Harvey in Texas? Was than not an omen for a new Noah to ready the ship?

It isn't true, as you state, that the secession of California was the cataclysm that opened the door. New York and Connecticut followed suit, and then Vermont. By the time Texas was out, there was hardly anything in, except Massachusetts. We stuck around and paid the price for it.

By 2020, when Trump tried to abolished Congress and dismantled the Supreme Court, we had all ceased to be citizens. Instead, we had become consumers. And we built ourselves to subsist as well-trained consumers. Countless ads told us what to buy in order to be happy, whom to vote for in order to feel secure, what news to watch in order not to distract our attention in "superfluous" endeavors.

Our diminished country is no longer a nation. Call it a conglomerate. Or a corporation. This depletion makes sense to me. The concept of Manifest Destiny was a way to justify the expansionist gumption of the nineteenth century. Big meant formidable. The reverse is true today: small is powerful. What nation wants to be imperialistic? The world's resources at a premium. The feeding of 400 million people is a never-ending task. Look at Switzerland, Costa Rica, and Ingrelia? The educational standard in each of these minuscule countries is enviably high and so is the standard of living. And Ingrelia, unlike the other two, has not disallowed immigration.

What exactly am I saying? That our dead shall not have died in vain, again. That bringing down Antifa monuments—in Amherst, of all places—is proof that the past is far more malleable than the future.

That I have trouble imagining a country still more idealistic than ours. Or more foolish.

What I don't have trouble with, my dear Editor, is seeing the literature that will spring from this great tragedy. Just as the First American Civil War produced great writers whose work was about much more than life in the battle—Harriet Beecher Stowe, for instance—our existential conundrum will turn ashes into gold.

I can already see a novel that in my imagination is called *Plexis* (2031) about the agony of losing one's relatives in the Covid-19 pandemic and then, alone in the world, wandering through deserted

American cities where death was at its prime, not because of the virus but as a result of fraternal infighting.

The scene in which the protagonist, Noah Rosenblum, engages the once prominent Black mayor, Bryan Wilson, who is now destitute, is incredibly moving.

Or the book-long epic poem *Toward April* (2029), in which our national language is reinvented in the opposite of Newspeak (I'm referring, of course, to George Orwell's *1984*), making it more elastic than ever, bringing to mind the linguistic effusion of a Zora Neale Hurston or a Henry Roth.

By the way, I remember reading years ago a passage in Ilan Stavans's book *What Is American Literature?* (2022) that American literature, unlike its counterpart south of the Rio Grande, didn't have *"una novela de dictador,"* a novel about a home-grown dictator. This is a shortage, in my opinion. Honestly, I can't wait to read one about Donald Trump's narcissistic reveries.

Maybe this is why America's Second Civil War was fought: so that a sublime literature could emerge out of it.

Is that ironic? We always thought life gave place to art. In truth, it is the other way around: we let ourselves live and die so that memorable narratives might emerge.

I've been a reader of American literature all my life. After finishing a book I deem significant, I've often wondered: What *is* American literature? How to conceive of it? My impression is that it is a looking glass. It reflects what it sees.

Enough, though. I long for the decades of prosperity between 1945 and 2020. Yes, there were repeated wars, such as those in Vietnam, Cambodia, Iraq, and so on. There was civil disobedience. There were assassinations like those of President Kennedy, the Rev. Martin Luther King, Jr., Malcolm X, Bobby Kennedy, etc.

Still, there was relative peace. Look what we have now: misery.

Yet I have hope. I will always have hope. Hope is America's currency, isn't it? I know I read that sentence somewhere.

Well, one more thought (hopefully without taking too much space in your "Letters from Readers" section): I love Robert Frost. I say this with absolute conviction. Although now he is mostly forgotten poet (another Dead White Male author in the dumpster), there was a time when people knew his verses by heart, chief among them "The Gift Outright."

In "A Cabin in the Clearing" (1927), a rather late composition, Frost writes: "Forgive, O Lord, my little jokes on Thee/ And I'll forgive Thy great big one on me." This is an extremely devout nation. I'm convinced that God does play jokes on all of us Americans. We have been fooled by Him/Her/They/It. We thought it was the other way around, didn't we?

Sincerely,

Your Dutiful Reader (Lt. Gen. Robert Chang Lee)

South Hadley, Massachusetts

INDEX

INDEX

ACKNOWLEDGMENTS

On July 2013, I published in the magazine *World Literature Today* an essay called "Is American Literature Parochial?" It brought along a controversial response. It was shared widely on social media, become the magazine's most read piece, and was assigned to classes and reading groups. My central argument is that under a façade of cosmopolitanism, American literature is rather insular. Some saw the essay as a diagnosis of larger national maladies. Others argued that the essay itself was a symptom of the problem it was seeking to describe and that the United States is a narrow, extreme, anti-intellectual, "fundamentalistic" country where everything is always looked at through a black-and-white prism.

The essay was followed, also in *WLT*, by another one called "Should Books Be Sold?" published on January 2014. There the argument rotated around the consumer nature of literature. We deem books successful if and when they sell. In contrast, books are judged to be forgettable, by which I mean disposable, if no pecuniary value is attached to them. That might happen even when they are in the market. This commercial approach to literature is about aesthetics only if aesthetics is seen as merchandise. My need to understand came from my teaching, my passion for books, and the fact that around that time I had founded a publishing house, Restless Books, devoted to the promotion of world literature in English translation.

Unconsciously, the two essays propelled me to think more broadly about national literatures and, particularly, about my own vision not of what American literature is but what it ought to be. And then, like a gift from heaven, came Donald Trump to convince me there is no better moment than now to think about the contours of naturalism, populism, tribalism, and other incessant maladies.

Other portions of the book originated in piece I wrote for the *New York Times*, the *Chronicle of Higher Education*, the *Boston Globe*, the *Los Angeles Review of Books*, and the *Hampshire Gazette*.

I want to thank Daniel Simon for his original invitation to write the essays in *WLT*. It was my friend Julia Kostova who after reading them imagined a larger, more sustained meditation. She contacted Jacqueline Norton, her colleague at Oxford University Press in the United Kingdom. It was my luck to fall into such intelligent, welcoming hands.

Norton was passionate for the project from the get-go, understanding its potential in the larger discussion on Americanness in the first third of the twenty-first century. Meeting at her OUP office, not far from where I lecture, at Sommerville College, for a couple of weeks every July, has been delightful. Our conversations over lunch helped me conceptualize the book's audience. I thank her wholeheartedly for wisely shepherding the manuscript through production. And for her unending patience as I, impeded by life itself, delinquently delayed the arrival of the final version.

As I was in the middle of writing, the major events in 2020 that defined the world—the Covid-19 pandemic and the shameful response to it by President Donald Trump, the collapse of the American economy, and the marches on streets from one coast to another, first after the death of George Floyd in Minneapolis, Minnesota, then once Trump sent federal agents to confront protesters in Portland, Oregon, and Seattle, Washington, galvanizing a population furious with the endless cycles of police brutality, and, finally, the splintering presidential election of November 3rd—focused my disquisitions on the capacity of literature to explain the nation's zeitgeist. This upheaval gave the book its gravitas. Norton encouraged me to anchor the argument in the present.

The anonymous readers of the proposal opened my eyes to my own misguided positioning as a critic. One of them in particular took me to task for foolishly describing myself, after twenty-five years in the public eye, as an outsider. The fact that I was born in Mexico and came to the United States at the age of 25 without much English had turned into a defensive mechanism in my consciousness. It was time to see myself as a sellout. Not fully. What makes the critic's voice necessary is its humming unhappiness. Giving that up means death.

I appreciate the conversations with Chris Abani, Paula Abate, Frederick Luis Aldama, Jon Lee Anderson, Christopher Benfy, Anke Birkenmaier, David W. Blight, Jules Chametzky, Jeremy Dauber, Ariel Dorfman, Daniel Donaghue, Lawrence Douglas, Boris Dralyuk, Regina Galasso, Henry Louis Gates, Jr., Daniel Gordon, Annette Hochstein, Jhumpa Lahiri, Josh Lambert, Jack Lynch, Anita Norich, Sherwin Nuland, Nathan Rostron, Max Rudin, Stephen Sadow, Ramón Saldívar, Peter Sokolowski, Werner Sollors, Doris Sommer, Edward Sullivan, Helen Vendler, David Ward, Diana de Armas Wilson, África Vidal, and the guests of the NPR podcast *In Contrast* and its executive producer John Voci.

ACKNOWLEDGMENTS

Throughout the years, Steven G. Kellman, at the University of Texas in San Antonio, has been my most supportive companion. It was thanks to an invitation he offered me to teach a class on misfits that I appreciated the quality of conformist nonconformity that American literature has been through the centuries. Kellman has been an invaluable companion in my intellectual journey. This volume is dedicated to him.

Gracias too to the stellar UK team of Oxford University Press. The manuscript was shepherded through production by Aimee Wright. It was copyedited by Timothy Beck. The index was prepared by Martina Martínez, alias M&M.

ABOUT THE AUTHOR

Ilan Stavans is Lewis-Sebring Professor of Humanities, Latin American and Latino Culture at Amherst College, the publisher of Restless Books, and the host of NPR's podcast *In Contrast*.